Youth H

Youth Homelessness

Courage & Hope

Edited by
HELEN SYKES

Melbourne University Press
1993

First published 1993
Typeset in Australia by John Sandefur
Printed in Malaysia by
SRM Production Services Sdn. Bhd. for
Melbourne University Press, Carlton, Victoria 3053
U.S.A. and Canada: International Specialized Book Services, Inc.,
5804 N.E. Hassalo Street, Portland, Oregon 97213-3644
United Kingdom and Europe: University College London Press,
Gower Street, London WC1E 6BT

This book is copyright. Apart from any fair dealing for the purposes of private study, research, criticism or review, as permitted under the Copyright Act, no part may be reproduced by any process without written permission. Enquiries should be made to the publisher.

© Individual contributors 1993

National Library of Australia Cataloguing in Publication entry

Youth Homelessness: courage and hope.

Bibliography.
Includes index.
ISBN 0 522 84572 X.

1. Homeless youth—Australia. 2. Homeless youth—Australia—Case studies. 3. Homelessness—Australia. I. Sykes, Helen (Helen Lesley).

362. 7083

Foreword

Peter Hollingworth, Archbishop of Brisbane

Ever since the 1960s I have worked with homeless young people. In those days we didn't give the problem a label, nor did we define 'youth homelessness' as a widespread social problem. Rather, it was regarded as a matter of funding somewhere for a few young people who had nowhere else to stay.

Mostly they had been thrown out of home, or had left after a severe family argument, or sometimes there was no viable family structure to support them.

As I think of it, the great difference between the 1960s and the 1990s is that this homelessness was viewed as an individual problem affecting a few. It was never defined as a societal problem of serious proportions. Since then we have witnessed a gradual worsening of things.

In the early 1970s agencies like Hanover Welfare services began to report that night shelter accommodation was being used by a growing proportion of younger people, with fewer numbers of the traditional older 'lone men' using the services. Even so, it was still perceived as a problem affecting individual young people.

In 1987 I was asked by the federal minister for Housing, Stuart West, to chair the National Non Government Committee for the International Year of Shelter for the Homeless. During that year we commissioned research into the various aspects of homelessness and inadequate housing in Australian society and then made recommendations to the federal government and the whole community. Even then, the problem of youth homelessness did not emerge as a matter of serious concern.

It was not until the Burdekin Inquiry had completed its pioneering work in 1989 that the phenomena was properly documented and the public was informed that at least 25 000 young people were homeless at any given time. The research showed that they were not 'young hoods' enjoying a free and easy, self–chosen lifestyle, but desperate young people who hated their circumstances and mostly wanted to find for themselves a secure safe future.

Frequently they had been physically or sexually abused by parents or by new de facto partners and they either left home in desperation or were thrown out.

The public initially was incredulous—how could such problems exist in these proportions when 70 per cent of Australians owned their own homes? The Burdekin Report was backed by a series of well-written media articles and some dramatic television documentaries which led to a new level of community awareness and understanding.

In remarkably quick time, community organisations and concerned individuals responded to what was clearly a widespread social problem. Out of such actions have emerged a number of well-conceived programs.

The Burdekin Report argued that housing for these young people had to be linked to training, education, employment and general community support facilities. The Federal Government responded with a program package involving an interdepartmental approach to the problem. As usual, problems occurred between levels of government and the response was slower than it should have been. It has, however, been strategically well conceived and will in time bear fruit.

Notwithstanding bureaucratic difficulties, the work must proceed on a broad community front, involving a wide range of agencies. Yet there is a sense in which everyone involved feels that they are still providing ambulances at the bottom of the proverbial cliff to pick up the victims after they have fallen. Still the problem remains as to how such human tragedies can be anticipated and prevented in the future.

Clearly, the main cause of the problem lies in the breakdown of family life and the loss of parenting skills. Domestic violence and abuse, so widely reported in the media today, are symptoms of something much deeper, related to the loss of human dignity and self-esteem.

Too often people enter into a relationship, have children and then split up, or have a child without the parental support of another partner, or drift from one unstable relationship to another. Perhaps too there are fewer grandmothers willing and able to take on another child as an extension of their family as often happened in the past. There are also fewer boarding houses run by tough but caring landladies. Perhaps too there has emerged in our society an ethos which encourages us to walk away from problems rather than stay and face them. When things are bad and family discipline and nurture has broken down, it is hardly surprising that so many children and young people become homeless and out of parental control.

If we had a clear set of answers aimed at solving such problems we would have acted before now. As a nation we have not even been able to establish a national family policy providing services to support, supplement or substitute for the family. One day such things will occur, and hopefully before the problem reaches epidemic proportions.

Meanwhile, the task must be tackled on many fronts. Mature people can be assisted in opening their homes, church and community groups can provide secure accommodation and more public housing must be made available to young people. They need to share housing, support each other and do so in an environment that offers access to further schooling, training and employment.

The tide of youth homelessness must be turned if we are to avert the problem of a growing underclass of excluded and alienated people who will live without hope and become brutalised and cynical. We must not allow ourselves to return to the tragedies of the nineteenth century industrial revolution by reintroducing the same problems in this post industrial age of ours.

This book goes much further than analysing and discussing the problem. It prescribes practical action, showing what has been done and what can be done. I commend it as an excellent school based community resource and I hope that it will be taken up and used in this way by many.

Contents

Foreword *Peter Hollingworth*	v
Acknowledgements	xi
Contributors	xii

Part One

1	Youth Homelessness and Schools *David Yencken and Helen Sykes*	1
2	Homeless Young People: Their Life Experience *Helen Sykes*	17
3	A School Program for Homeless Students *Helen Sykes*	32
4	Communities Working Together *Helen Sykes*	47
5	The Role of Schools: Learning from the Ardoch Experience *Helen Sykes and David Yencken*	65

Part Two

6	The Dilemmas of Youth Homelessness *Rodney Fopp*	77
7	The Social Costs of Youth Homelessness *Robyn Hartley*	100
8	Economic Benefits of Supporting Homeless Young People *Daryl Dixon*	121
9	The School, Youth Homelessness and the Future *Jan Carter*	129
Bibliography		145
Index		153

Illustrations

between pages 72 and 73

Housing Support
Volunteer Support from the Broader Community
Support from School Staff and the Ardoch Youth Foundation
Ardoch Graduate now in a teaching role
Sharing Environment
Students at the breakfast program

Acknowledgements

The inspiration for this book came from the homeless students at Ardoch-Windsor Secondary College who had the courage to tell the general community about their life experience in the interest of helping *all* homeless young people.

I wish to thank the students from Ardoch, who participated in the case-study for the book for their willingness to share their experiences with me. I also wish to acknowledge the participation in the case study of staff from Prahran Secondary College and the people from the broader community. They are leading by example with their commitment to and support for homeless young people.

I would also like to express my appreciation to Peter Hollingworth, David Yencken, Rodney Fopp, Robyn Hartley, Daryl Dixon and Jan Carter for their generous contributions to the book, and to Carlos Alcaide, the photographer. All of the contributors have donated their time in order to assist homeless young people continue with their education. Proceeds from the sale of the book go directly to the Ardoch Youth Foundation.

Contributors

Jan Carter

Jan Carter is Professor and Head of the Department of Social Work at The University of Melbourne. She was previously Director of the Social Policy and Research Centre of the Brotherhood of St Laurence. Professor Carter has an extensive background in social work in Australia and the United Kingdom. She has been a principal researcher at the National Institute for Social Work, London, and a visiting fellow at the Australian National University, the University of Western Australia and Murdoch University. Professor Carter was a Commissioner on the National Inquiry into Homeless Children conducted by the Human Rights and Equal Opportunity Commission.

Daryl Dixon

Daryl Dixon is an economics graduate of Queensland and Cambridge Universities. He was formerly Head of the Policy Co-ordination Unit and the Social Welfare Policy Secretariat in the Commonwealth Department of Community Services and is now a private consultant. His report, The Costs of Child and Youth Homelessness, forms the basis of a chapter in *Our Homeless Children*, the Report of the National Inquiry into Homeless Children. Daryl Dixon advises the Brotherhood of St Laurence on economic and social welfare policy issues. He is the author of several books including *The Social and Economic Costs of Unemployment.*

Rodney Fopp

Rodney Fopp is Chairperson of the Sociology Department at the University of South Australia. He has been investigating the housing problems facing young people for over a decade. His report, Homeless Young People in Australia: Estimating the Numbers and Incidence, forms the basis of a chapter in *Our Homeless Children*, the report of the National Inquiry into Homeless Children. Dr Fopp is co-author with Dr Cecily Neil of *Homelessness in Australia—Causes and Consequences.*

Robyn Hartley

Robyn Hartley is Research Fellow with the Australian Institute of Family Studies. Her areas of research interest are youth policy, relationships between young people and their families, the transition from adolescence to young adulthood, and youth and family homelessness. Robyn Hartley's publications include, 'Issues arising from the implementation of the Youth Homeless Allowance', 'On the outside: the needs of unsupported, homeless youth', 'What price independence?: a report of a study of young people's incomes and living costs' and 'The social costs of inadequate literacy: a report for International Literacy Year'.

Peter Hollingworth

Peter Hollingworth is the Anglican Archbishop of Brisbane. He previously worked with the Brotherhood of St Laurence, for the last ten years as Executive Director. Archbishop Hollingworth has been an outspoken commentator and critic on social justice issues. He has written extensively and made contributions to numerous committees on these issues.

Helen Sykes

Helen Sykes is a sociologist working as a consultant to the private and public sectors. Her areas of research interest include environmental and urban attitudes of young people in Australia and internationally, and youth homelessness. She is currently researching the needs of at-risk secondary students. Dr Sykes is a Board Member of the Ardoch Youth Foundation.

David Yencken

David Yencken is Professor and Head of the School of Environmental Planning at The University of Melbourne. He has previously been the Chairman of the Australian Heritage Commission, Australian Government, and the Head of the Ministry of Planning and Environment, Victorian Government. Professor Yencken has served on many other government bodies including the Australian National Commission for UNESCO. He has recently carried out research on urban and environmental attitudes of young Australians.

Part One

1

Youth Homelessness and Schools

Most people would agree that 'there is nothing extraordinary about young people leaving home. It is one of the expected transitions to adult life' (O'Connor 1989: 1). Most people would also believe that this transition can be a difficult one. But very few have understood that the change from childhood to adulthood has been traumatic for some children, because they have had no home and because they have been forced as a consequence to live in the most degraded and exploited circumstances. The homelessness of young people has been an invisible problem in Australian society. In this book there are several examples of the dismay and disbelief that individuals have felt when first confronted with the experiences of homeless children. Typical is the reaction of Kathy Hilton, Welfare Co-ordinator at Prahran Secondary College: 'When Eloise came to me she was coming to school from the Brotherhood bin. That's how desperate she was. I had not been confronted with homelessness before. It just shocked me.'

Our Homeless Children, the report of the National Inquiry into Homeless Children (Burdekin Report), prepared and published by the Human Rights and Equal Opportunity Commission, did much to destroy that complacency (Human Rights and Equal Opportunity Commission 1989). It stripped away the social veneer covering the extent of youth homelessness and the experiences of homeless children. It documented these experiences vividly in the words of the children themselves. It also documented the inadequacy of government and community responses.

Since the release of the Burdekin Report there has been a new urgency generated about the needs of homeless young children. There have been many reports on the subject. 'A Summary and Analysis of the Burdekin Report' (Dwyer 1989) has, for example, been circulated to youth workers. The Victorian Council of Social Service has published a review of the federal and Victorian governments' responses to the report (Victorian Council of Social Service 1990). The Commonwealth Government has published a report listing the new Federal and State services that have been introduced in response to the Burdekin Report (Department of Health, Housing and Community Services 1992). Other detailed analyses of homelessness in Australia have been carried out. (Neil and Fopp 1992).

This book aims to contribute to this general debate; generating awareness of youth homelessness remains a critical problem. The book, however, concentrates on a particular aspect of youth homelessness, the role of schools. Schools are recognised by the Burdekin Report as having an important part in the relationships homeless children have with society. The report catalogues the many ways in which schools have failed homeless children, as will be described later in this chapter. Schools can, however, play a much richer role than has been recognised in any of the literature. Our book examines this potential, using some inspiring examples as case studies.

What do we Mean by Homelessness?

Although at first it might not seem so, homelessness is a complex phenomenon. It can be defined broadly or narrowly, objectively in numbers and concrete experiences or subjectively as the perceptions of individuals, as a personal and family problem or as a problem of the structure of society. Both the analysis and the proposed solutions vary according to the definition used. This will be a recurring theme in the book.

We also have to ask what we are dealing with. Is it shelter alone? Is it providing a home in a more generous sense of the term? Is it food or income to buy food? Is it love and caring and emotional support? Is it access to education and other opportunities for learning the technical and social skills needed for a satisfying and productive role in society?

How might Homelessness be Approached?

Many of the children interviewed for the Burdekin Report had no shelter. 'Nowhere to go, nowhere to sleep, nowhere to have any meals or nothing' (Tom). '... living on the streets. Hardly no food at all. Nowhere to go. No shelter... living in squats off the streets' (Jack) (O'Connor 1989: 22). Tom and Jack are homeless in the literal sense of the word. This is the popular understanding of homelessness, being without adequate shelter.

Providing the shelter is a need that anyone can recognise, but does it provide a home? It needs little imagination to see that shelter alone is not enough. This is Petra's definition of homelessness:

> When you don't have anywhere to live or you have got somewhere to live but it's not a place of your own. You get chucked around every week from one place to another and you're really totally relying on other people. You've got no money of your own. You probably haven't got your own room and you're just travelling around all the time looking for somewhere more permanent. (O'Connor 1989: 20)

Petra has shelter but no home. How should we then define a home? The attributes of home could be seen to be:

- security of tenure;
- security for each member of the household against internal and external threats;
- physical characteristics which do not undermine health or compound other disadvantages such as poverty or disability;
- affordability;
- the possibility of living with individuals of ones choice;
- privacy; and
- control and autonomy. (Neil and Fopp 1992: 3, 4)

This is a much richer definition of home. All of these are very important attributes of home and objectives that we should undoubtedly aim for. There are, however, difficulties with such definitions. They leave themselves open to the response that a definition of homelessness as the absence of any one of those attributes would mean the categorisation of a significant percentage of the population as homeless. It might further be argued that a widely embracing definition would dissipate the sense of urgency needed to deal with the plight of those who are most in need. This difficult issue of homelessness is explored in greater detail in the second part of the book. For the purpose of this part of the book, it is enough to recognise that providing shelter alone is not an adequate solution to homelessness and that many of the attributes of home listed above do have to be satisfied if a sufficiently stable home environment is to be created to enable homeless children and youths to find a minimally satisfying place in their societies. In the book there are several examples of children who have found or been given housing which has met their shelter needs but has been quite inadequate in other ways. Often this housing has exacerbated their problems.

Is it food or income to buy food? The picture painted of homeless children in the Burdekin Report and from interviews in this book is one of enduring poverty, malnourishment and sometimes starvation. Half of the children interviewed by O'Connor for the Burdekin Report had previously been charged with criminal offences. Some of these offences may have been related to drugs and other addictions but most evidently related to a lack of money to feed and support themselves. As O'Connor observed, ' . . . these young people lacked sufficient sums of legitimately obtained money' (O'Connor 1989: 11). Providing the income or providing the food thus has to be included in any package of measures designed to solve the underlying problems of homelessness.

Is it lack of love, caring and emotional support? It is very difficult to talk about the lack of love and caring. Such a discussion might too readily seem trite and superficial. Providing love and care would also seem to most people hopelessly beyond the scope of any community response. Yet to Kathy Hilton at Prahran Secondary College it is the critical issue. She would say that it is lack of love, care and emotional support that has particularly characterised the experiences of homeless children; that it is this lack that has forced the children out of their homes and led to many of their emotional and behavioural reactions. She would further insist that a response to children's homelessness that does not include a means of providing the emotional support that has been missing throughout their lives is a poor response indeed. It would be very difficult to argue with her.

Is it access to education? Dropping out of school is the typical experience of homeless children. But education is one of the most important escape routes out of poverty. The relationships between the levels of education and employment, described, for example, in the Australian Bureau of Statistics data on the unemployment rates of young people according to educational qualifications, show that employment is closely related to educational achievement. The lower the level of educational achievement and the earlier the departure from school the greater is the likelihood of unemployment.

The school has another very important role to play. Homeless children evidently have no stable family or home environment. Where can they find any form of substitute? How can they be expected to gain skills, find jobs and lead fruitful lives if they have no stability in their backgrounds? It is hard to think of a more suitable place than the school. The school does offer the potential of a stable and supportive environment; school involvement is an extremely important way, often the only way, for homeless children to maintain contact with normal society.

Our argument is that an effective response to youth homelessness has to deal with all of these dimensions of homelessness. Unless it does, the answers will be partial at best and the chances of emotional rehabilitation, access to the work-force, and escape from poverty, crime and exploitation will be very poor. By any measure, the personal, social and financial costs of such a failure will be very high.

Many will baulk at such a comprehensive program, at its scope and cost and at the great difficulty of its implementation. This book will, however, show that the task is not so enormous or impossible and that there are existing programs which have found answers to all these problems. The crucial role in all these examples is that of the school.

Other Dimensions of Homelessness

Before turning to a more detailed discussion of the role of the school, there are two further issues of homelessness that deserve to be noted. The Burdekin Report observed that the analysis of the underlying causes of youth homelessness might be approached in two different ways. These causes could be seen as related to problems of individual families and social relations or as related to structural problems of society. The authors of the report note their agreement with the submission made to the inquiry that 'both views had a great deal of credence and what was needed was a sense of balance' (Human Rights and Equal Opportunity Commission 1989: 85). In its conclusions and recommendations, however, the report concentrated significantly on measures to help families, provide income support and find accommodation—that is, on issues of family and social relations.

The report has indeed been challenged for this emphasis. Dwyer, for example, has observed that the report missed the opportunity to show the links between social and economic policies, that it evaluated social needs in terms of their economic costs but failed to evaluate economic policy in terms of its social cost (Dwyer 1989: 9). Dwyer went on to say:

> The gap between rhetoric and practice in the area of child welfare is directly attributable to this assumption that economic policy can be effectively evaluated independently of its social impact. Social policy is relegated to the sphere of 'rhetoric' because economics is assumed as the only real concern of 'practice' Thus, social needs or costs become a 'background' consideration or even a mere 'afterthought'. The moral outrage which colours many sections of the report runs the risk of being identified as part of the rhetoric of welfare.

Homelessness is also a particular problem for women. Studies have shown that homelessness of men is much more visible than homelessness of women (Watson 1986). The individual experiences described in the Burdekin Report and in this book show that girls and young women are particularly vulnerable to abuse and exploitation and that their special problems must be seen as aspects of the structure of society as much as of personal and family relations.

Further, homeless young people are not simply helpless victims. They find ways of coping and adjusting often with courage and cleverness. These adjustments may be fully or partially effective means of dealing with extraordinary stress, but they may also lead to crime or anti-social behaviour which in its turn may create many new problems for the young people concerned. They may make access to housing more problematic; they may make re-entry into mainstream society very difficult indeed (Neil and Fopp 1992: 9).

These issues of youth homelessness are discussed in more detail in the second part of the book. They provide the context in which the role of the school must be viewed.

Why are Schools so Important?

Schools can and often do contribute to the problems of child and youth homelessness. Reviewing the statements of homeless children interviewed as part of the research project for the National Inquiry into Homeless Children, O'Connor observed that 'for most of the young people interviewed their school experience was not a happy one. The process of marginalisation, rejection and exclusion experienced in their families was also reflected in their school experiences (O'Connor 1989: 85). O'Connor found that the young people interviewed had, almost without exception, severed their links with their schools before they had completed grade 12. His conclusion was that the school system had failed these young people as much as had other institutions of society.

O'Connor (1989: 85–93) specifically found:

> *There was little time for those who had difficulty in coping.*
> 'I left school because I couldn't do the school work and no one was willing to help me.' (Sybil)

There are problems with relationships with peers.
> 'Kids at school were ripping me off because I had um, just because I was large and had a reading problem, they didn't want to know you; they think: "Go to hell, you're stupid you don't know anything." (Sybil)

There are conflicts with school authorities.
> 'Got in fights with teachers when they started picking on them, shit like that. See, that's why I went on the Alpha Course, well, 'cos I hit a teacher.' (Jim)

Problems at school lead to problems at home.
> 'I got kicked out of school, and then I got kicked, two days later I got kicked out of home for getting kicked out of school.' (Dennis)

Family difficulties in their turn create difficulties at school.
> 'The education system in High School is geared to them and their situation of being at home with a family, whereas with me I don't have that family support, either financially or emotionally and um I sort of feel like a square peg in a round hole, um, sort of the way the school is run.' (Laura)

Leaving home creates special problems for those in school.
> 'I was kicked out of that school and then I went to another school nearby and then I went to another part of Melbourne and . . . ' (Ian)

The school often did not respond to the problems of young people's difficulties at home.
> 'Like a lot of them just thought, she's only a kid, a silly little kid, exaggerating with everything. I never trusted adults very much in my life.' (Carol)

Those interviewed identified many important barriers to returning to and staying at school including: lack of stable accommodation, school assumptions that students have family support, the school's lack of understanding and flexibility in accommodating homeless young people, the clash between the lifestyle of homelessness and the lifestyle imposed by school's expectations, young people's perception that school was irrelevant to their daily lives because of their daily struggle for survival, lack of resources and the stigma of homelessness/institutionalisation. The report concluded that 'it is an indictment on the school system that . . . young people do not identify the school system as a potential source of support and assistance' (O'Connor 1989: 90).

Support from Schools

The Burdekin Report also recognised that the school had the potential to assist homeless youths and children. It particularly noted the scope available to the school to identify and respond to difficulties faced by homeless children, to monitor violations of the rights of children and to ensure that their rights to an education are met (Human Rights and Equal Opportunity Commission 1989: 73). This book will also argue that the school has a special role to play as an institution with which all homeless children have some association, as a potential source of social contact and stability and as a means of personal and social rehabilitation.

The school experiences described in the Burdekin Report and its associated research are not, moreover, the only forms of relationships between homeless children and schools. Some schools and their communities have responded admirably to the challenge. One such school has been Ardoch-Windsor Secondary College. Ardoch has been chosen as a case-study for the book because it shows how a school can deal with all the issues identified earlier in this chapter. It particularly shows what can be done if the school environment is of the right kind, if there are dedicated, committed and caring people in the school, if there are effective support services provided by other agencies and if there is help of all kinds from the outside community. Ardoch is also particularly significant because of the number of homeless young people that have been enrolled and retained in the school.

Ardoch student support program

Ardoch-Windsor Secondary College came into being in January 1988 with the amalgamation of Ardoch High School and Windsor Technical College. In November 1992 the school was closed as part of the program of school rationalisations carried out by the new Victorian government.

The Ardoch student support program began in 1988 not as a conscious act of state or school policy, but rather as an individual response to a slowly growing awareness that there were children attending the school who had no homes, horrifying personal experiences, serious physical and emotional needs and who were in consequence facing very significant educational problems. Over the next four years, the program developed and took shape. Since the student support program began with the first student Eloise in 1988, the number of homeless students at Ardoch-Windsor College increased significantly each year. There were 12 homeless students in 1989, 48 in 1990, 78 in 1991 and 102 identified as homeless in 1992. To the authors' knowledge, this is the largest number of homeless students to be found at any school in Australia.

When the incoming Victorian Government announced its intention to close Ardoch, those involved in the student support program, including the Ardoch Youth Foundation, initially set out to find money to keep the school running in order to preserve the program. In the event, the staff directly involved in the program were transferred to Prahran Secondary College. Students previously attending Ardoch were given the opportunity of enrolling at Prahran. At the commencement of the 1993 school year, there were 72 homeless students and 100 students at risk of becoming homeless enrolled at Prahran Secondary College. The program appears to have transferred smoothly and successfully, the principal and staff at Prahran have provided a supportive environment and the Ardoch Youth Foundation activities are all working to help Prahran students in much the same way that they had previously done at Ardoch. Because Prahran is a larger school than Ardoch, it appears to offer some additional benefits to homeless students since it may be it easier for those students to integrate into the school without being so identifiable as a large proportion of the school population. The larger school is also able to offer a wider range of subjects and skills. Whether these initial promises will be fully realised and whether the program continues to flourish and develop will of course require a longer experience in the new school environment.

Ardoch Youth Foundation Inc.

The Ardoch Youth Foundation was incorporated in November 1992. The members of the foundation are from the Ardoch school community and the broader community.

The primary purpose of the foundation is to provide funding and channel community support for programs that assist young people who are homeless or likely to become homeless to continue with their education. Assistance is available to all schools without discrimination.

The Ardoch Youth Foundation aims to assist schools throughout Australia in setting up programs modelled on the student support program developed at Ardoch-Windsor College. The foundation also aims to raise awareness in the community about the needs of homeless and at risk students.

Many of the people involved in creating and developing the student support program now operating at Prahran Secondary College are also board members of the foundation. Several of these people, Kathy Hilton, Eloise Tregonning, Graeme Wise, Vaughn Clare, Tony Conabere and Julie Rothbart, tell their stories in the first part of the book.

Other school initiatives

The Ardoch program is not the only program of its kind in Australia nor is Ardoch (now Prahran Secondary College) the only educational institution to help homeless young people in school and with their schooling. Here follow some other Victorian examples.

Wespact Youth Project

The Wespact Youth Project was initiated in 1989 by Mrs Sadie Stevens (the current chairperson) in response to publicity about youth homelessness surrounding the Burdekin Report. Mrs Stevens felt that young homeless people, 'were on a merry-go-round of various agencies and something had to be done to break the cycle. Any program to help them had to see past just providing shelter'.

The Wespact Youth Project provides support with accommodation, continuing education and training. Support is provided in the form of regular house meetings and homework assistance. The target group for the project is young people aged 16–25 years who are homeless or at risk of being homeless.

The project, which is located in Footscray (a suburb of Melbourne), is able to provide accommodation for eight young people in its three houses. Ms Jen Millar, the project's Housing Officer, advises that the project would like to support more homeless young people because 'there is a crying need for more accommodation and support. Financially it is extremely difficult for these students.'

A free tutoring service in maths and English is also provided in seven different locations in the Foostscray area to support at risk students. Ms Vivien Archdall, the Education Liaison Officer at the project, explains: 'We see many students who find it difficult to study at home because of things like constant family arguments or too many children in the house.' Many of these students have non-English-speaking backgrounds. Vivien Archdall says, 'The students we are helping now have a very positive attitude because somebody cares, somebody listens and somebody is interested in what they are doing'.

An important role of the education liaison officer is to sensitise local schools and the community about issues surrounding youth homelessness.

In 1993 three students assisted by the project commenced tertiary studies. Two of these students are attending university and one is at TAFE.

The project is jointly funded by Community Services Victoria, Supported Accommodation Assistance Program (SAAP) and the Victorian Education Department, Students At Risk Program (SARP). The project is conducted under the auspices of the Faculty of Human Development, Victoria University of Technology,

Brotherhood of St Laurence

In the last six months of 1991 the Brotherhood of St Laurence conducted an action research project *Learning to Survive* (Morris and Blaskett 1992). Six Melbourne metropolitan secondary schools participated in the project; Ardoch-Windsor Secondary College, Clayton/Huntingdale Secondary College, Collingwood Secondary College, Maribyrnong Secondary College, Preston East Technical School and Upfield Secondary College.

The research was designed to study the financial and support needs of a group of homeless students and to examine what additional factors might help them to complete their schooling successfully. Thirty-two homeless students (all were receiving AUSTUDY) from these schools participated in the project. Half of the students received a regular supplement of $32 per week and the other half were given access to an emergency fund. The students' financial needs were documented in a diary of income and expenditure over a two-week period and through individual and group interviews. Details of support available to homeless students were recorded through interviews with school staff and people from relevant government offices. Relevant literature was also studied.

In addition to financial assistance, the students were encouraged to take an active part in raising issues about student support and in finding solutions. A program of co-operative advocacy was developed on their behalf. A holiday program was also created in response to a need strongly expressed by students during the program. 'This project has demonstrated that there is a large and growing group of young people who amaze themselves, their teachers and others who know them by trying to complete their schooling while living on what is probably the "lowest" living income paid in Australia' (Morris and Blaskett 1992: xi).

The project illustrates the struggle homeless students have trying to support themselves while completing their secondary education and emphasises the importance of adequate financial assistance. The project report urges governments to provide proper support services in schools and allowances to enable homeless students to capitalise on the benefits of education.

South Oakleigh Secondary College

The supported accommodation service provided at Clayton/Huntingdale Secondary College referred to in the Brotherhood of St Laurence report, has now been changed to South Oakleigh Secondary College Youth Housing Project. Mr Geoff DeCruz, the Youth Housing support worker, advises that both students and non-students use their service. The year after the *Learning to Survive* research project carried out by the Brotherhood, the service had 205 young people (students and non-students) referred to it. Geoff DeCruz reports that in the first two months of 1993, 47 young people were referred to the project. He added, 'These statistics indicate the need in the community for supported housing for young people'.

Maribyrnong Secondary College

The Homeless Students Project at Maribyrnong Secondary College has provided support for a significant number of students from non-English-speaking backgrounds. The Student

Support Worker, Mr John Byrne, explains that the help needed by these students is made that much more complex because of language and cultural differences.

Mr Byrne believes that the Homeless Students Project has created a recognition in the community that, given the right amount of support, homeless students can function and survive in a school environment. 'They gain a feeling of self worth and success, not just in an academic sense. School-based support does make a huge difference.'

Home Project

The word HOME stands for Holding On to My Environment, Esteem and Education. On 17 March 1993 the Home Project was launched at Box Forest Secondary College, Glenroy (a suburb of Melbourne) by Mr Brian Burdekin, the Human Rights and Equal Opportunity Commissioner.

The Home Project is a community initiative supported by the William Buckland Foundation. The project aims to develop an integrated community response to young people at risk of becoming homeless, based on the early intervention role of the school. It has as its premise that alienation of young people can be prevented if their difficulties are identified and acted upon as early as possible.

The Executive Officer of the project, Mr Alec Gunningham, explains:

> The inspiration for the project came out of concern from people in Glenroy about the disturbing number of homeless young people who were early school leavers. The Project embraces the philosophy that the broader community also has a role and responsibility to support young people. The community is defined as the schools (there are four campuses involved), community agencies, clubs, industry, government departments and residents in the local area.

The project involves an evaluation team of academics from three different faculties at Victoria University of Technology. Team members are: Marty Grace, Social Work, Delwyn Goodrick, Psychology and Maureen Ryan, Education. Prior to the commencement of the project, the team conducted preliminary surveys to identify the needs associated with homelessness in the community and to develop understandings of the best ways of meeting these needs.

Lack of information

These examples illustrate a growing recognition of the crucial role played by schools. There is, however, little systematically collected information available on programs of these kinds in Australian schools. In Victoria there appears to be no information available on the numbers of homeless young people enrolled in schools, let alone information about young people at risk of becoming homeless or who have already dropped out of the school system. This lack of information is a serious impediment to the development of more effective school based programs.

The other striking thing about these examples is that each is a local or community response to a growing awareness of an important social problem. None has come into being as part of a government-inspired program.

The Structure of the Book

This first part of the book reports on the findings of a study conducted by Helen Sykes during 1992 and 1993 of the support program for homeless students at Ardoch-Windsor Secondary College and Prahran Secondary College. The following three chapters tell of the experiences of some of the students and of the people involved in developing and conducting the program at Ardoch and Prahran schools. All of these experiences are told in the individual's own words. The individual stories illustrate how young homeless people respond when they have the opportunity to regain control over their lives, develop real choices and make decisions.

The names Kathy and Mike are frequently referred to. Ms Kathy Hilton is the Student Welfare Co-ordinator at the college and Mr Mike Loughman is the Youth Worker.

The students participating in the study were self-selected on the basis that they had the confidence to explain their life experiences starting from their earliest memories. For all of these students, there were many painful moments as they retold experiences of rejection, poverty, parental neglect, physical abuse, emotional abuse, sexual abuse and severe family conflict. In some of the stories told here fictitious names are used to protect the identify of the student.

In chapter 5, Helen Sykes and David Yencken reflect on the Ardoch/Prahran experience, on what can be learnt from it and on the way these learnings might be applied to other schools.

The second part of the book focuses on the more general policy and theoretical aspects of homelessness and homelessness programs for young people. Rodney Fopp explores the many dimensions of the problem, including causes and possible solutions. Robyn Hartley examines the social costs of youth homelessness for both individuals and the community. Daryl Dixon surveys the economic costs of homelessness and the economic benefits of supporting homeless youths, emphasising the advantages of assisting them to achieve through education. In the concluding chapter, Jan Carter comments on the initiatives that are currently being and might in the future be taken by governments, educational institutions and individuals in Australia to support young people who are homeless and at risk. The recurring theme throughout the book is the role of schools.

Commonly, theory, public debate and policy have been based on the needs and problems of homeless young people who have already left school. It has been assumed that these homeless young people have had little interest in continuing their schooling. The role of schools has therefore played little part in the debates. Both at a theoretical and research level, the issues concerned with support for homeless youth who want to return to school or to continue with their secondary education have not been adequately explored.

The purpose of the book is to redress this balance and in doing so to show how schools can make a major contribution to the problem of youth homelessness.

2

Homeless Young People: Their Life Experience

Eloise (21 years old)

My parents separated when I was about 4. It was a real struggle for my mum to support my brother and I. I was very conscious of the poverty from a very young age. Even going on school excursions was a real issue. We were too scared to ask mum for money. Not having the coolest clothes was also difficult. My father never paid mum any money for us and she was always under pressure to pay bills.

My mother was lonely and didn't have any adult support around her. She used to drink too much wine. My mother was emotionally disturbed and when she was drinking she used to take it out on me.

Because I was the oldest I took on a lot of responsibility for my younger brother. It got to the point that I could see that things weren't right at home. All the responsibility was too much and I couldn't handle it any more. I was then 14 and achieving very well at school.

I went to live in Queensland with my father for a year and that was an absolute disaster. He carries a lot of guilt. He smokes dope so he is stoned most of the time. I did year 10 in Queensland and I was getting straight As. I was made to feel in the way. My father just didn't want me there.

I started using drugs in Queensland and then when I came back to Melbourne I went straight into it. I ended up using speed and cocaine. I was basically just numbing myself. From an early age I can remember just wanting to die. There is the feeling of helplessness, of no way out, of always being caught in poverty.

Because I was so young, drug users would let me stay with them. I wasn't sleeping with them but I was like a pet dog. I would sell drugs in night-clubs for them. That was the exchange. I was selling it, I had somewhere to live and I was getting it for free.

When you are using drugs like that you are on a death trip. Part of the drug use is wanting to die but there is some sort of hope involved with it.

When I came back to Melbourne nothing had changed with my mum and I became homeless. I took my brother with me because I felt I couldn't leave him with my mum. I was homeless from about 14 to 17 years and the people I was around in that time are either dead, in jail or in mental institutions. It is the poverty and the day-to-day existence that drives you crazy. You feel like a rat in a cage. You are not even part of society.

Somehow part of me knew I was going to get out of it because I was so determined. I believed that there was a better life.

I enrolled at Ardoch when there was no homeless program. I just started to go to school because I saw education as the key to my future. When I went back to school I was crashing out on the street. You only crash out on the street when every other alternative is not there.

There have been many times in my life when I haven't had a cent for months and I have survived. There are so many caring people in places like the Salvation Army and the Brotherhood of St Laurence. Through meeting other homeless people, you work out the whole system. You work out your whole survival. Part of my survival on the streets was my intelligence. I was a master at lateral thinking.

When I came to Ardoch I realised it was the last straw and if it had not worked I am pretty sure I would be dead now. It was the last connection with society and any institution. My sense of worth was pretty dismal but I kept holding on to a belief that things would be better. I started in year 11 at Ardoch. The teachers are on a first-name basis and the environment is casual. There are teachers who are truly there for you. I was putting a lot of blame on myself for the situation I was in. Part of me felt really ashamed and guilty for my mum.

One day I told my art teacher that I had nowhere to go. I was so used to it that I really didn't realise how insane the situation actually was. My art teacher could not believe what she was hearing. I was the first person to confront the school with the problem of homelessness. From that point on, Ardoch has been giving young people the opportunity to get out of the vicious cycle.

I feel great about myself now. Year 11 was difficult detoxing my body. It was so easy to slip back because it was an easier road. I made a commitment that I was going to get out of the situation I was in and go to university. Having that big picture made me go to school every day.

Kathy was definitely there for me like my mother couldn't be. Having someone who can advocate with government for you and someone who has their heart in it for you is so important.

I did well in year 12 and got into Melbourne University. I now mix with people from all walks of life. I don't feel any different or any stigma. Now I am part of society and the possibilities for me are endless.

I see myself in a facilitating role and speaking to people about change. Part of me feels obligated for the opportunities I have been given. I feel that I must do something about the problems of youth homelessness and poverty.

When I was young and caught in the poverty trap, I had no concept of love. It was a whole cycle based around guilt and fear. I definitely have a concept of what love means now. This has come from working on self-esteem. Having Kathy in my life and having people love me has really got me in touch with loving other people.

Fiona (14 years old)

When my parents broke up, my mum gave me and my younger brother to my dad as he wanted us more. My father died of a heart attack a few years later when I was 7. I was asleep next to him. I then went to live with my mum and there was a lot of fighting. I have three step-brothers and one step-sister.

When I was with my dad things were really good because I was really loved by him. I didn't get on with my mum. She was very jealous of us kids and my father. She always liked to have all the attention, everything for herself.

When I lived with my mum after my dad died, there was a lot of fighting. I didn't do very well at school because I found it hard to get along with people. I had so much unhappiness at home that the way to get it out was at school. It was sort of an escape at school.

When I went to secondary school my mum sent me to live with my grandmother. When I returned we still kept on arguing so I moved out. I don't have any contact with my mother now. She doesn't support me in any way or try to make contact with me.

My brother from my father keeps contact with me all the time. He doesn't get on with my mum but he is too scared to leave. She is supporting him, in a way to get back at me. My brother and I ran away several times but things never changed.

My mum used to sleep around and I didn't like that. I was still young and she would spend more time with her boyfriends than her kids. We were emotionally neglected although we were properly clothed and fed.

When I left home, I just stayed at my friend's place for a while. I wasn't comfortable with other people supporting me so I came to Kathy and Mike at Ardoch. I had no one else to tell because at the time I was having trouble with my stepbrothers as well. Kathy helped me out.

After my father's death I found out that my step-brother and step-sister were sleeping together. My step-brother was also sexually abusing me. I couldn't talk to any one about it because he made me afraid to. He tried to bribe me. There was nothing I could do about the sexual abuse.

Now I try not to think about it. I told my mum about the sexual abuse but she didn't believe me. My mum got a new boyfriend and he supports her. She just felt that she had to satisfy her needs and not worry about us.

Kathy talked to me about the sexual abuse and organised a counsellor to talk to me.

I thought being homeless was freedom and independence with no hassles. When I got into that situation it was different. I didn't choose to leave home but I had to.

Plenty of times my friends have said, 'use drugs and you will forget your problems'. But you don't they are still there. I found it difficult to escape.

When I was sexually abused at 8 I didn't know what it was. I also used to walk in on my mum having sex with these different men. My mum just acts like a teenager. She used to be into alcohol and drugs.

I felt loved by my father. I didn't feel loved by my mother. I was well brought up by my father, I had manners and was well disciplined. My mother just said 'do what ever you like. I just don't care'.

I want to finish my VCE and go to university. I want to make something of myself. No member of my family has gone right through secondary school and to university. I think staying here at Ardoch is going to make the difference between succeeding or not. There is always someone there at Ardoch. The teachers are terrific.

Ardoch could help heaps of kids who are in situations like me, but they are too scared to say anything. There is always that fear about where am I going to stay and what am I going to eat.

When we give speeches at other schools we tell the kids about our experiences. At one school this guy came up to me and said he thought I had heaps of courage.

I am still seeing the school counsellor and that is helping with the things that have happened.

Kerrie (17 years old)

I was adopted. We lived in the country and life was pretty good. My mother died of cancer when I was 10. Then my family just broke down.

After my mother died, my father said you are basically on your own. He said he would provide money and shelter. My brother who was also adopted kept bashing me up. My father said he couldn't do anything about my brother and that it was up to me. So I left home when I was 15.

I am really angry at my dad because he just didn't want to face his responsibilities. He would come home after work, drop all his stuff and go out. He would not even speak to me. He would also go out all weekend. I had to look after myself completely. I had no idea of personal hygiene. I ate junk food all the time and I was overweight.

I had very low self-esteem and I didn't care what happened. I went to two private schools and I wasn't allowed to have problems at those schools. I told a counsellor and she said 'that's normal, that's okay, don't worry about it'.

I came to Ardoch and the counsellor here said there was something wrong. Before that, I thought what was happening to me happens everywhere.

I wasn't achieving at all when I was with my father. I was rebelling.

I still have low self-esteem but it is getting better. I can now assert myself to do things, especially at Ardoch because there is no pressure. I know I have to apply myself and that's what I do.

I still have a few problems. Sometimes I just want to be my age. I am sick of doing things my friends don't have to do like paying bills and looking after the house. Sometimes it really gets me down and then other times I think this is really great. I have learnt to do these things early.

When I first came to Ardoch, I was taught what was right from wrong. They helped me with food, money and clothing. It is very rare that we have milk or bread in our fridge, that is a luxury for us.

The breakfast club is a good way to start the day. All my friends go and we cheer each other up. It doesn't feel like charity.

Kathy and Mike are just like my family. They were sort of like parents for a while. If I had any problems I could go and ask their advice. That was really important to me.

The program at Ardoch is helping so many people do things for themselves. It is not just providing food and shelter it is actually providing education. Before Ardoch I had this feeling that I was totally stupid. Now I know I can do it.

I go to other schools and talk to students to tell them what happens at Ardoch. We really show the kids that we are not street bums and that we don't drink all night. We tell them that we are achieving things. At one school the kids said they were expecting yobbos.

Peter (16 years old)

We were living with my grandmother. When she died, we moved to another suburb. Mum remarried and I had problems with my stepfather. He just doesn't understand me. My stepfather wants me to be smart and straight.

My father died two years ago. I only got to know him when he had cancer. I became real close to my father and then he died.

I just can't talk to my stepfather so I just stayed in my room.

My mother just went crazy one night and hit me with a pot and told me to get out. My sister is on drugs and she got bashed. My mum is stressed out.

I am living in a flat with friends and it is working out.

Ardoch is providing me with $30 a week until I get AUSTUDY. I am confident that I have enough skills to look after myself.

The previous school I went to was too strict for me, too religious. I was telling my friend about my problems and he said to talk to Kathy, so I did. Kathy helped me out a lot. She gave me money for food and she is helping me to get AUSTUDY.

Being able to talk to Kathy has been important. My friends also help me sort out my problems. At Ardoch the teachers and kids are friendly. I feel everyone is equal here.

I go to the breakfast program. The food is good and I like the company.

Now that I am not living at home I feel more responsible. My friends are making me come to school which is good. I am going to study hard now because I want to be a plumber.

Beth (19 years old)

I was adopted when I was one year old. Until the age of 16, I was sexually, emotionally and physically abused. The physical and emotional abuse came from my parents. I was sexually abused by my uncle. My parents knew about it and they told me I was crazy. They said it was my fault to let it happen. I didn't know it was wrong. I thought it was normal.

I didn't know it was called sexual abuse until Kathy told me. I was 16. Then my whole world changed physically and emotionally. I lived on the streets. I was an alcoholic and I tried to commit suicide.

Now I am in year 12 and I know I will pass my studies.

I don't have anything to do with my family now. I live on my own in a flat. Sometimes I feel alone but I can speak to Kathy and Mike.

I want to study nursing to deliver babies because I was dumped in an orphanage when I was one. I am bitter about being left in an orphanage.

Last year I was raped and I went to a sexual assault centre. Before that I had men of fifty and eighty sexually abusing me. I am now seeing a psychiatrist to deal with being sexually assaulted.

I just try and put the past out of my mind now. I try to concentrate to the best of my ability to prove to myself that I am not crazy or stupid. I try to be really determined.

The breakfast club is good because you get a meal and it makes you feel energetic during the day.

Kathy provides a shoulder to cry on. She is there for me. People have hurt me a lot. I don't want to be hurt any more.

I have been at Ardoch for three years. Without the support program, I don't think I would be at school. If I wasn't at school, I would probably be unemployed, an alcoholic and living in a Salvation Army house. I went to Alcoholics Anonymous and I can drink in moderation now.

The important thing for young people who have had bad experiences is to break the cycle.

Jim (21 years old)

I never really got on with my dad. We sort of fight. My mum tries to compensate for what my dad takes away and just makes it plastic. I end up getting nothing. My parents fight a lot.

My father is a real fascist man. He likes to dictate what has to be done and how things are to be done. I don't agree with that and I never fitted into a slot. I wanted to do music and art and creativity stuff. He is into wanting me to be a doctor or a lawyer and I never fitted into any of that.

I could have achieved at school but I didn't want to do what my father wanted me to. We used to get into arguments when I was younger and he used to knock me around. When I got older I used to fight back. He knocked me out once. I didn't really talk about it when I was young. I used to get really angry and get really drunk a lot. I was 14 or 15 then. Looking back now he probably did the best he could, but it didn't mean much to me when I was a kid.

I was 15 when I left school the first time. One day I just packed up my bags and left home. I left my parents a note saying I couldn't live up to what they wanted. I went to a friend's house in the suburbs and then I just started sleeping in the streets in the city. I was hanging around and drinking. I busked with my guitar. Sometimes I crashed in a hostel for the night or at friends' houses.

I didn't have much concept of the word love. I feel loved now but not by my parents. Recently I have had a few emotional problems giving up drugs and drinking and some people at Ardoch have helped me out. I feel loved by the teachers and kids at Ardoch. It makes me feel confused.

I used to take heaps of drugs when I was 16 and it sort of screwed my brain about a bit. I sort of lost touch with reality a bit for a couple of years. I gave up ten months ago but I still get the effects of it. I haven't had a drink for the last seventeen days which is probably the longest I have been without a drink in the last five years.

When I was on the streets I just flooded myself with people. There is always heaps of street kids and that makes it a lot easier. You just sit up and joke and get drunk and then it is all cool. I got a bit sick of doing nothing and taking joints all the time. We used to sell drugs to get the money. It wasn't to make a profit but to cover what we were taking. I had a bad time on the streets with drugs and I came to the realisation that I had to do something.

I came to Ardoch and started enjoying it. I am doing year 12 now and passing everything. I have been turning up heaps and I am enthusiastic about my subjects. Ardoch gives me stability and the love that I get here is important.

I just haven't experienced dealing with emotions so I have tended just to walk out and go and get drunk. I don't want to deal with things in the past but things in the future. I want to succeed in life now.

I didn't like myself when I was on the streets. I knew I could do things if I wanted to. I thought that all society had to offer was a 9-to-5 existence. I know that society has more to offer now. I want a house in the country and to have kids. I love kids. I would like to help other people who are going through similar experiences.

When I started at Ardoch I was pretty closed off from people. I have trouble communicating my emotions when I have problems. I sort of broke down a bit. When I turned up to school, I was wrecked and I was getting really sick. I wasn't living anywhere really, I was just floating.

I now share a house which Kathy organised for me. I have a house where I feel safe. I have my room that I can put my personality into.

I taught myself guitar and I am good enough to make a bit of money from it. Music and art are my main releases. My father doesn't like my art or my music. He thinks they have no value.

A friend of mine killed himself when he was 14. My father saw that as weak. I thought it was sad that a 14-year-old wanted to kill himself. When I was about 15 I tried to kill myself a couple of times.

It makes me feel good that there is a school like Ardoch for people. My friends and the teachers at Ardoch make me feel that I have a lot to give. They make me feel that I am smart and a good person and that I don't need to get drunk. I still have trouble with other people thinking that I am okay.

Mary (20 years old)

When I was 7 my mother died of cancer. It was just after my brother was born. A woman my father had been having an affair with when my mother was sick moved into our home the day after my mother died. I felt very badly about it. We had to move because my dad didn't want relatives to get me and my brother.

My father's girlfriend destroyed our mother's things. She burnt the diaries our mother had written for us when we grew up. The girlfriend stayed on and off.

My father died in an accident and it was pretty bad because there had been a lot of tension between my father and me. Before my father died, I was raped by a close relative who was looking after us. I told my father and he was pretty apologetic. He made sure I went to counselling.

After my father died, the girlfriend put me on tranquillisers. She didn't let us go through the normal grieving process. She refused to let us go to my father's funeral.

For six months we were shuffled around from family to family until custody was awarded to our maternal grandparents My grandfather is an alcoholic and incredibly violent. I left after twelve months. I then lived with several different members of my family. It was good at the beginning and then I was made to feel unwelcome.

I have always been a good student when I had a stable background. Unfortunately that has not been very often.

One night I was staying at a friend's place and I got quite drunk, I had an alcohol dependency problem. I woke up to find him raping me. I became pregnant and I had to arrange a termination. Alcohol was largely an escape. I used to drink in the school bus in the morning.

When I was 16 I got a job as an apprentice chef and then became a full time-trade chef. I started using speed to keep me up for work. That escalated to two or three hits a day. I don't have any great hunger for it any more. I find it very hard to see young people using it and to shut up and let them work it out for themselves.

I also had a problem with sleeping pills and tranquillisers. Because of insomnia and the depressive cycle. I can avoid that now.

Ardoch has meant that there is a stable base for me to work from. It means that I can continue with my studies without feeling destitute due to rental subsidies.

I am making my point to the community with public speeches. The point I want to make is that being homeless is not the scum of society. We didn't ask for it to happen. We don't want pity, we want understanding. I want to get off welfare.

Now I am more centred with plans for my career. I know my strengths. I want to do nursing and if I don't get in, I will do year 12 at Ardoch.

People who have been through the experience of homelessness are supportive to other people. You don't have the patronising effect that a lot of social workers create.

Christine (20 years old)

I lived in the outer suburbs. My parents divorced when I was 6. They swapped looking after us, depending on who was having the bigger nervous breakdown.

Dad was always out. There were big drug sessions at home with my dad and his friends. My dad didn't know how to look after kids. It was just an insecure way to live. My eldest sister left school when she was 15 and took over as a parent for us. She didn't know how to do it much so we weren't really cared for.

I can't remember liking school. I was very stressed at school. If you go to school and you don't have nice clothes to wear you really feel horrible.

I was being sexually abused from about 8 to 12 years of age by my dad's best friend. I know my self-esteem was very low. I had a lot of trouble relating to my peer-group. I was always really afraid and insecure. I was sexually abused by my father once when I was 14. I think one of my sisters was also sexually abused by my dad.

I used to go to school stoned from the after-effects of all the drug smoking by my father and his friends. They used to smoke so much and I would be around it all the time. I didn't do very well at secondary school. I didn't know I could do better then.

When I was in year 9 I moved in with my mum and I went to another school. Things started to improve. I realised that I wasn't dumb but I didn't think I had any academic ability.

In the area I grew up kids are just factory fodder. There isn't many options.

I became pregnant at the start of year 11 and stayed at school until the middle of the year. I stopped seeing the father of the baby when I was two months pregnant. He was a recovering addict, which is pretty normal for me.

I have never taken drugs and I think that was because of fear. When I was young at least every second house dealt in drugs or used drugs to excess. It was everywhere.

My mum always had a lot of problems. She was an alcoholic and she was always having a nervous breakdown. Now she is in a major depression.

From 15 I was promiscuous. I could relate more comfortably with men if I had sex with them. The promiscuity was lack of discipline and not of knowing how to relate to people of the opposite sex. This came from watching people around me who were promiscuous. Or just nuts, violent or abusive. I look at sex differently now. Now it is a decision based on good feelings.

I came to Ardoch because I want to get my VCE. I want to make something of my life. I want the security of not being stressed about money. The teachers make the difference at Ardoch. They believe in you. The people at Ardoch are really positive about my ability. People who I think are smart like me. I don't feel the need to speak indiscriminately about the sexual abuse. I am starting to realise that I have a lot to offer. I know I will pass this year.

At Ardoch I get lots of help. I just get op shop clothes for myself. I always dress my son very nicely. That is very important to me because I wasn't dressed well as a kid. There is emotional, material and financial support at Ardoch if you need it. Ardoch has given me self-worth and, once it starts, it snowballs as much as the bad stuff. I am doing better now and my marks are improving.

I know that I am a pretty good mum. I am making sure that my son is not around alcoholics and drug addicts.

A lot of people think of homeless kids or kids with disadvantaged backgrounds as scary. I went to a private school to give a talk and one kid asked me what I ate. I asked him what he ate and he said steak and stuff. I told him that I eat more vegetarian but that I also eat steak.

When I was at my previous school I picked up the way other people spoke because I wanted to speak well, not rough and coarse. I know it is an advantage, an asset. My son's vocabulary is very good too.

John (26 years old)

I came to Ardoch because I didn't I have anywhere to go. I also made a decision to work in the theatre.

I was adopted. I was the middle child and the only one adopted. When I was 11, my adoptive parents separated and there was a lot of tension in my high school years. At the end of year 10 I left school and within six months I had left home as well. I was unemployed on and off for three years. Between the ages of 16 and 18 I didn't speak to my parents. My parents were disappointed in my achievements at school and when I was working. They would ask me when was I going to get a real job even though I was doing lighting and design in the music industry.

I am in year 12. I get AUSTUDY and just get by. I make all my own clothes and I go to the breakfast program at school. I just wouldn't be able to afford breakfast at home. During the holidays, I have one meal a day at lunch-time.

There is a huge range of students at Ardoch. A large percentage of the school population has been through some sort of difficulty and there is a bonding together. The counselling here means that there is someone taking an interest in me as an individual with no judgements.

I had an alcohol problem when I was working for bands, two bottles of scotch a day. It was so readily available. Now I am creating my buzz out of life naturally. I now feel good about achieving. The high comes out of self-achievement. I can manage my emotional situation now.

When I finish at Ardoch I want to come back and help with the program. The Ardoch program only scratches the surface of the needs that are there with homeless young people.

Carol (19 years old)

For the last half of my life I have been verbally and physically abused by all the members of my family. My two sisters were bashing me to relieve their stress and anger. My mother was mentally torturing me and my father was physically abusing me.

I was very confused and I didn't know why I was always in trouble. I stayed in my room for long periods because I was too scared to come out. The first time I told someone about what was happening to me was when I was in year 8. My friends were worried about me because I was always crying and very depressed.

I had also tried to kill myself. Then my school co-ordinator became someone to talk to but she never helped me. She only told me not to hurt myself so I shut my mouth. I didn't talk to anyone so they came to the conclusion that everything was fine. I was too depressed to care any more.

By year 12 I was beginning to take drugs because I needed an escape from reality. I could not take any more. My friends supported me and I left home in the middle of the year. I moved around a lot and I was never sure where I would spend the next night. My parents hired a private detective so I would always be looking over my shoulder.

After three weeks of sleeping at friends' places, I went home and tried to go back to school but it didn't work. At that stage I was at the end of the line waiting to die.

I spoke to the chaplain at school. He helped me to get into a St John's safe house. The people at the house helped me a lot. After about a month I found myself a flat.

I knew I had to go back to school to give myself a better future. I enrolled at Ardoch. Kathy and Mike helped me buy the necessary books and they put me into counselling. I owe them a lot. Ardoch has helped me more than any private school I have been to.

Joan (19 years old)

Since the age of 11 I have had a disrupted family life. My mother and father split up. I stayed with my father and helped him look after my younger brother and sister.

I missed out on a lot of school because I was looking after the family for three years. It all got too much.

I went to live with my mother. She had many boyfriends. I was often left alone and I was scared. Eventually she married a violent, alcoholic man who used to abuse her while I was watching. I was very scared.

I was made to feel guilty for everything that was happening. My mum chose to stay with my stepfather. I couldn't stand it any longer. I left my mum's house.

By this stage I was severely depressed and my schooling had suffered enormously. I changed schools and came to Ardoch My father had moved interstate without leaving any forwarding address.

The school finally found me accommodation. I'm now settled in a student flat with support from the school.

Settling down has been traumatic for me. However, now I feel confident as an independent student.

I don't want to be on the dole. I feel I can make something of my life.

3

A School Program for Homeless Students

The Problems of Homeless Students

Kathy Hilton

The school environment

I came to Ardoch at the end of 1987. I came as a teacher to a very caring school. The philosophy of the school was to treat all students as individuals. There was a feeling of acceptance. Nobody was labelled as dumb. The philosophy of the school came from all the staff.

There was a whole range of kids at Ardoch. Some people chose to send their kids to Ardoch because of the philosophy of the school. Everyone seemed to accept each other.

Teachers were on first-name basis if they chose to be. It was an individual decision and I think it broke down barriers.

It was recognised that a lot of the kids needed a family-type atmosphere. The school was in an experimental stage with vertical classes being conducted where appropriate. Pastoral care operated on a home-group system.

Although the kids were happy at school, they would go home with nothing much changed. A lot of the kids' problems were not being addressed and there was no trained person on staff who that could deal with that. There were guidance officers visiting Ardoch once a week. However, it was only the really naughty kids that talked to the guidance officers.

Student Welfare Co-ordinator

In 1988 a Student Welfare Co-ordinator position was established and because I was qualified for the position I took on the job. Being a humanities teacher, I always found ways of responding to the kids' interests, everything was okay to talk about. I listened to the kids and recognised that they had problems. I always spoke to each kid at least once throughout the lesson. The kids needed to be known and valued. The kids could also approach me outside the classroom and discuss their problems.

It was difficult establishing the position because kids don't know who to trust. Some kids have been very hurt by the people they have dealt with previously. If the focus is on behavioural things, the kids won't come and talk about their problems. The rest of the staff were important in encouraging the kids to talk about their personal problems.

The word got around the school that it was okay to talk to me, that I was fair, non-judgemental and treated them with respect. Kids brought their friends to see me. Gradually an atmosphere of trust was built up.

Working in the classroom has been important because I experience the kids as a group and the other teachers know that I understand classroom dynamics.

During my counselling experience, I assisted kids who were victims of domestic violence, poverty and unemployment at home, but I had not confronted homelessness as an issue.

The first homeless student

At the end of 1988, Eloise, a year 11 student, came to me with a problem. She was homeless. When Eloise came to me, she was coming to school from a Brotherhood bin. That's how desperate she was. I had not been confronted with homelessness before. It just shocked me because I had heard of homelessness but I associated it with overseas. It was not a societal issue that was known, talked about or that people were prepared for.

Because I had never had any experience with homelessness, at first I didn't know what to do. From day one, it was a learning experience. I didn't think it would be as hard to help

Eloise as it actually was. She was fed, clothed and provided with school books from our personal resources.

The issue of youth homelessness

Students who were labelled as no hopers and ended up homeless could have been picked up a lot earlier.

Homelessness with Eloise and a lot of other kids who have come to the school has been the end result of a process. Although every story is different and deserves to be looked at individually, in my experience homelessness is generally the result of traumatic family breakdown. Some of the common reasons for family breakdown I encounter are ongoing domestic violence, incest, alcohol abuse, drug abuse, unsupported mental illness, poverty and unemployment. The word ongoing has to be underlined. Very rarely does a child run away and become homeless after a single incident of being hit.

All the kids tell me that they left home because things were pretty bad at home.

Bad means different things to different kids but it is usually abuse of some sort.

Young people tend to make excuses for what has happened to them. For example, a kid who is the victim of an alcoholic would explain that he beat up his wife and child but only when he was drunk. During further discussion, the kid would explain that father was drunk four or five times a week. The kid would add that it was the alcohol that made him do it; it wasn't his fault.

Youth homelessness and school

The homeless young people haven't always wanted to be at school. For a lot of the kids, school has been a negative experience since primary school. Some of the kids were made to feel that there was something wrong with them because their parents couldn't afford decent clothing or didn't look after them properly. These feelings were internalised. When these young people talk about their experiences at traditional schools, it is not with a lot of affection.

The homeless kids may realise that going back to school is the only way out of poverty but they do not want to return to the traditional system.

Development of the student support program

In the second year, we had twelve homeless students and Eloise was still not appropriately placed. All twelve of the kids were hungry so we suddenly had a lunch-time program. Some of the kids were from squats so we allowed them to shower and wash their clothes at school.

There was no stigma attached to the students who were homeless. They were treated as individuals and there was an acceptance of their individuality. Ardoch was a non-uniform school. This was important because it allowed the kids to express their individuality through their clothes.

At all stages we let the state and local governments, VCOSS, the Brotherhood of St Laurence and the Salvation Army know what we were doing. They were all interested in what we were doing. The Brotherhood and the Salvation Army wanted to work together with us in a partnership role. The Salvation Army acknowledged us as an important resource for homeless youths. They were a great support. Ardoch was a pioneer for meeting the needs of kids who wanted to stay at school or come back to school. The needs of the young who were at risk of being homeless or falling out school were also addressed. We had kids who had lost their jobs because of the economic situation coming back to school.

The myths were broken. The myth that homelessness was a choice, the myth that homelessness was a life of freedom, the myth that there was nothing that could be done to prevent it and the myth that these kids didn't want to be at school.

For example, with the rent subsidy, we found that with a little money we could provide housing with dignity and choice.

The support program at Ardoch developed as a direct response to the needs of the young people. Because the program made a difference and was successful, in many ways people's attitude to homeless young people has broadened.

Ardoch was different. The word got around that homeless kids would be supported at school and there would be understanding. Students at risk are also supported to catch them before they are on the streets.

The many elements of the support program have developed in response to the needs of homeless students at Ardoch. In summary, they involve: housing, health care counselling, advocacy with government departments, lunch and breakfast programs, curriculum support, pantry of food, store of second hand clothing, store of toiletries, store of furniture, a crisis fund, a part-time holiday employment project and a public relations program.

Government response

I thought there would be experts to take over from me and take responsibility for looking after the kids. We let the Education Ministry know very quickly that we had a homeless kid at the school. I was excited that we had a homeless young person who wanted to be at school and thought that the Education Ministry would do something to help. I had firmly believed the rhetoric on social justice and equal opportunity, and on the need to raise retention rates at schools. Wherever we went in the government, we were told that it was some other department's responsibility. Meanwhile, the homeless person was hurting and suffering. Everything to help homeless students was in the pipeline. The pipelines were really long and we couldn't wait. The needs were immediate.

We had to look for emergency housing for Eloise. The system that was available was horrifying. Students were afraid to go into emergency housing because of all the problems. Kids were screaming and yelling, things were being stolen and junkies were on the premises. Often our students would rather spend the night in the park than go into that sort of accommodation. Recently, there have been changes in emergency housing for kids.

At that stage, there was no recognition that homeless young people would want to be at school or that there might be homeless youth who would attend school if they had the support to do so.

At times I was at my wits end to know what to do. They were young kids and some were failing their classes. Often they couldn't get to class because they were so tired. But with every blockage came a new way. We just kept looking for new solutions. We were forced to create different options, some better than others.

Government-supported accommodation

At this stage, there was a recognition that some young people needed supported housing, but the waiting list was long and the kids went through trauma being interviewed. It could be months before a young person was placed in a house. We didn't accept that.

After a couple of months, we got Eloise into a supported housing project run by local government and Community Services Victoria. There were seventeen people for every one spot on the list. However, at the project there was no acknowledgement that anyone would want to go to school. We had to provide proof before it was taken seriously.

Eloise was put into a house to share with a drug pusher. It was worse than being on the streets in many ways. There seemed to be a feeling that a roof over a young person's head was enough. There was no furniture provided and no one in the house had any. Eloise was shifted and the next place was also inappropriate. She was sharing with an unemployed young girl who partied all night and a depressed young girl who wouldn't get out of bed in the morning. There tended to be a feeling that Eloise was strong and that she could help the others. Her needs were not recognised.

We kept pushing for student-specific supported housing. We went to our local council, St Kilda Council, and they were really terrific at that stage. They had a youth officer who came to the school to see how the council could help. We demonstrated to the youth officer that there was a need for student-specific housing options. This resulted in a proposal for a student-specific housing option being developed by Ardoch and the council. The proposal was put to the state government in October 1989. A delegation including Gordon Harrison, the St Kilda Council youth officer, Peter Wearne from the St Kilda/Elwood Theos, Brian Corbett, principal of Ardoch, three Ardoch students and myself met with Joan Kirner, the Minister of Education. The outcome was the establishment, over twelve months later, of the St Kilda/Prahran Student Accommodation Program. There were forty-eight homeless students at Ardoch by the end of 1990 and the government provided only two flats.

The government's response to the proposal took so long to become a reality. It was expensive and it only gave us four beds to share among three local schools.

Blocks

The homeless young people opened a new world for me. I became frustrated with the government system because of all the blocks that were put in our way. When we were assisting Eloise, we had to deal with seven different departments. There was a definite lack of co-ordination. It was obvious to me that the government needed to take a new approach to youth homelessness.

I soon realised that I knew how to do something to meet the needs of the homeless kids at Ardoch. I was able to help them because I cared enough about these kids to really listen to them and then respond.

I had students sleeping on the floor of my counselling office. I was trying to have school buildings opened for kids to sleep in. The government wouldn't let us use school buildings because that was a legal responsibility. I tried a lot of different things and found a lot of blocks. Squats were illegal but, at some stages, even a squat looked good because at least the kids would have a roof over their heads. Kids were telling me stories of staying in night-clubs until 7.00 a.m. just to have shelter because they didn't have anywhere else to go. The emergency accommodation system was full to the brim.

Response to the Burdekin Report

After the Report of the National Inquiry into Homeless Children by the Human Rights and Equal Opportunity Commission came out in 1989, Ardoch was recognised as a school that was doing things to respond to youth homelessness. We were encouraged to continue. The Students At Risk Program was set up by the federal government as a pilot project. The Victorian Ministry of Education developed seven pilot projects as part of the Students At Risk Program. The Homeless Students Co-ordination Project was one of the Victorian pilot projects. Ardoch was one of four schools recognised as providing support to homeless young people and invited to participate in the project.

In the first year of the project, Ardoch received $18 000. At that stage we had forty-eight kids identified as homeless at Ardoch and I couldn't handle the workload. We used the money to employ a youth worker. In addition to the forty-eight homeless students, there were many other students who were at risk of being homeless. Because it was a caring school it attracted more kids with problems that needed addressing.

The funding from the Students At Risk Program has continued at $18 000 per year. However, there has never been any certainty about when the money would arrive and if the funding would continue. The other problem is that there have never been any clear guidelines given about how the money could be spent.

Response from the broader community

I have listened to the students and learnt from them. Other people have also learnt about homelessness in this way. It has always been a team effort. The mission has been to spread the message about the realities of youth homelessness for all the young people.

We spread the message mainly through public speaking and the media. Whenever we explained the situation of the homeless students at Ardoch, barriers were broken down and there was understanding and action. We were able to create a larger and broader family of supporters because the people we spoke to wanted to do something.

The first public talk we gave was in 1989 at Mount Scopus College, a private co-educational secondary school. I was joined by Eloise and another student. The teachers and students cried when they heard what was happening. They did a walkathon for us that year and raised $750.

We couldn't use vacant school buildings and we couldn't use squats. It is very difficult for homeless kids to rent a flat. Understandably people are reluctant to lease a flat to young people who are not good prospects. Some were too young to sign a lease. Finding the money for the bond and the first month's rent is also difficult for young people who are homeless. For some young people, even rental subsidies aren't enough. We had to find a solution.

I suggested that the school itself rent a flat to house some of our homeless students who had no housing option. The principal of Ardoch, Brian Corbett was very supportive and, when we found a flat for two girls who had been living in a squat, he signed the lease. The money raised by Mount Scopus paid for the bond. We also subsidised the rent by $30 a week. We initiated rental subsidies. No one had done that for homeless students before. The only semester the two girls passed while they were at Ardoch was the semester they were in the flat. When the Ministry of Education found out, they issued a directive that it was illegal for the principal to sign the lease and that we couldn't do it. Schools were not to sign leases.

This was another block created by the system. However by this time I knew I could find a way around it. I decided to find someone outside the education system to sign the lease.

The second flat was funded by Odyssey for two of their girls who wanted to return to school.

By this stage other people were asking what they could do to help. We were invited by ANZ Trustees to participate in a talk with Brian Burdekin the Human Rights and Equal Opportunity Commissioner. Four students and I spoke and after the meeting John Bell, managing director of Esprit, offered to help. Esprit funded the third flat.

The community responded to the publicity we got and many interested people visited the school. The support program for homeless students at Ardoch has became widely recognised in the community.

An important part of the program at Ardoch is raising awareness of the realities of youth homelessness and the needs of students who want to continue with their education. Mike and I, together with groups of students, have addressed schools, media and interested community groups.

We have spoken at conferences in Launceston and Brisbane. There has also been a lot of interest from professionals located throughout Australia in the Ardoch student-support program. They are keen to know how we are responding to the needs of homeless students. We like them to visit the school and speak to the students.

Ardoch brought welfare into the school and challenged the traditional role of education. The support program for homeless students is now being widely recognised.

Ardoch has not been officially recognised as a disadvantaged school although in 1992 it had the highest number of homeless students in the nation.

Success

Success for the kids at Ardoch is measured in many ways. Some of the students have gone to university, some to TAFE and many have got jobs. For some of the young people, success is passing one or two subjects at year 11 or 12. It has given them a whole new look at themselves as many of these young people had dropped out of school as early as year 7 and 8 as so-called failures. For others, success is the fact that it is the first time they have been surrounded by caring people.

Sometimes kids don't start achieving until after they leave school. I recently received a letter from a young lady that left school under very unfortunate circumstances. This is what she wrote:

> I am writing to apologise for the way I treated you and Mike after you had both done so much to help me. I feel thoroughly ashamed.
>
> The past six months have been a period of transition for me. I am seeing a sexual assault counsellor and, with their help, I am finally achieving what for years had remained just out of reach. Drugs no longer take top priority in my life.
>
> I have the best news: this year I am doing a social work degree. I would like to be a youth worker.
>
> You have been a tremendous influence on me and I have a great amount of respect and admiration for both you and Mike. I doubt I would have shown it but at the time I lacked the qualities to respect, love and be honest with myself. Now I want to improve my reality and that involves facing up to all the problems I ran away and hid from.
>
> I want to be able to give love and support, sound advice and actual assistance to the many people who have no-one else. I would particularly like to work with adolescents. I feel I maybe could relate to kids with problems more easily than had their experiences from a text book.
>
> Though I made it harder than it had to be I still achieved my goal and learnt many valuable and painful things. Thank you for all you did to assist me.

We have provided role models for our homeless kids. The kids can receive and give love now. Even the ones who have dropped out have remembered years later what happened at Ardoch. We have also provided opportunities for people who have wanted to help.

Hearing that the school was being closed down made members of the school community and the broader community value what they had at Ardoch. The kids realised they really cared about the people at the school and they didn't want to lose them.

We still provide housing assistance for some of the Ardoch students who did not enrol at Prahran in 1993. For curriculum reasons it was not appropriate for these students to enrol at Prahran.

Mike Loughman: The Youth Worker

Team support

When I came to Ardoch in 1991, there appeared to be two distinct groups of students we were dealing with. There were the kids who were homeless and needed accommodation and support and the kids who weren't homeless but were out of home a lot and at risk of becoming homeless.

In general the homeless kids had dropped out of school for a couple of years and for a variety of reasons had come back. They had hardships with accommodation and money, but they had motivation. The kids at risk had hardships at home and generally lacked motivation. The homeless kids tended to be older.

My role was to give Kathy support and to add the youth work focus to the support program. This involved networking with welfare agencies in the area. I worked inside and outside the schools.

Structured housing program

The first thing I did was focus on the housing side of the program. We looked at linkages with youth housing programs to see how they could be used effectively. When we got kids into the youth housing program, my role was to visit the premises and set them up properly. I was like a housing worker and visited the flats once a week. Kathy and I together dealt with rental issues including collecting the rent. Kathy found each of the flats and organised the sponsors. We went from one flat when I came to Ardoch to six flats when we moved to Prahran.

Over time, I helped Kathy to develop a more structured housing program. I worked on documentation for the housing We produced leases and agreements and formalised the interviewing. Working in a formalised structure was important because the kids could see what was expected of them. The kids were accountable for paying the rent and looking after the flats. Previously everything was done on trust which allowed some people to exploit the situation. Exploitation was part of the lifestyle of many of the kids.

During 1992 we developed a pilot program with Hanover Welfare Services because there was not enough time for me to be a housing worker, be a resource to teachers and help the kids. We were always responding to crises instead of doing prevention and support work.

There was an obvious need for a full-time housing worker We didn't have the funds and there was no way that the government was going to fund a housing worker for Ardoch.

The pilot program which started at the end of 1992 involves Hanover employing a housing worker to deal directly with students from the school and directly with Kathy and me. The housing worker at Hanover now collects the rents and looks after the flats. Kathy and I do the emotional and school support work with the kids in the flats. This arrangement works better for us and the kids. Now when the kids leave school, if they have the resources, they can buy out the lease of the flat.

Areas of concern

At Ardoch over 50 per cent of the students were working with Kathy and me. There was also a fear that Ardoch was becoming a dumping ground for homeless and at-risk kids. I believe that it is important that these kids are integrated with other types of students. Because Ardoch had an image of being a dumping ground, some parents weren't prepared to send their kids to the school. Ardoch was known as a school for non-achievers, which labelled all the kids.

The Transition to Prahran Secondary College

Russell Harrison

Principal's perspective

The profile of the students at Prahran Secondary College is about 70 per cent non-English-speaking background. There has been an increase in Chinese students and recently an influx of Russian students. Ardoch had a markedly lower non-English-speaking background.

A lot of the Ardoch kids knew the Prahran kids through social interaction and primary school.

With the transition to Prahran, the Ardoch students have stayed in the same area. Now Kathy Hilton is one of two people sharing the student welfare co-ordinator role and Mike Loughman is the youth worker. Julie Rothbart runs the breakfast program here now and supporters from the broader community such as Graeme Wise and Vaughn Clare attend the breakfast program at Prahran. I encourage people from the broader community to come into the school and support the homeless and at-risk students.

I hope the professional people from the broader community who are contributing to the student support program will also be able to add some skills to the school council.

Welcoming attitudes

Once the decision was made on 20 November 1992 to close Ardoch, mechanisms were put in place by the Prahran school community to encourage the Ardoch students to move to Prahran. I invited the people who were running the student support program at Ardoch to visit Prahran to see how we could make the program work at Prahran.

We asked the Ardoch students what subjects they wanted to do in 1993 and we expanded the curriculum to accommodate them as much as we could.

The contribution of the Ardoch program

Prahran already had a student support program covering a broad range of services. We had lunch vouchers and at various times we provided breakfast. We also had students living in flats provided by the Prahran and St Kilda councils. This was the project initiated jointly by Ardoch and the local council. We didn't have anywhere near the same number of homeless and at-risk students as at Ardoch.

The students at Prahran are benefiting by having these support services expanded. The house where Kathy and Mike are located is used for student counselling and storage of food and clothing for the students. There is a washing machine and a dryer for students to use; it is a base for the Ardoch student support program.

The breakfast program in its new home at Prahran seems to be highly successful. It is attracting around 100 kids each morning. Both the Ardoch and Prahran students are going to the breakfast program. It a place where they can also make their lunch for the day.

I see a vibrancy among the Ardoch students who have come to Prahran. I think for too long, the City of Prahran perceived Prahran Secondary College as the ethnic school with the relative straight curriculum and Ardoch-Windsor College as the school that was more involved with art and drama. I believe it is in the best interest of all the students to have the benefits of the strengths of both schools.

The transition of the Ardoch students will take time and it is by no means easy. It is happening at a time of severe cuts by the Directorate of School Education. We now have a broader cohort of students to look after. For example, two single mothers came from Ardoch; we are meeting their accommodation needs at Prahran.

Mike Loughman

Benefit of moving

There are many benefits for the Ardoch kids being at Prahran Secondary College. The 100 kids from Ardoch are in a school with a population of 500 students. There is far more variety for the kids. There is a more diverse range of students and there are a lot more migrant students. The school has some extra resources. For example, Prahran has a school bus for kids to go on camps. I think Prahran will be good for the younger kids because they can continue to get necessary support and all the school activities. The structure of Prahran doesn't allow kids to cop out.

Prahran has extensive school sport, a camping program and a school atmosphere. At Ardoch sport was non-competitive.

The other benefit of the move to Prahran is that Kathy and I now have a house opposite the school that will be open during school hours and school holidays.

I feel the Ardoch kids are settling in and recognising the benefits of being at Prahran.

One of the things that is making the move for the student support program work is the willingness of the Prahran principal and teachers to have Ardoch kids at the school. The principal has put a lot of work into promoting the acceptance of Ardoch kids.

Referrals are now coming for housing for Prahran kids. The Ardoch kids who are comfortable with Kathy and myself are telling their new friends at Prahran about us. I think the student support program will be broader at Prahran. We will be able to help more students at risk.

We give kids an option and there are some kids that run with it all the way. There are some kids that exploit the options. If they want to succeed, the supports are available in the program.

One of the important things about the student support program is the development of a model that other schools can pick up and run with.

Kathy Hilton

Continuity of care and support

When we started the new year at Prahran, a boy who had been on the streets for a long time returned to school. Matt is only 15 and he has been rejected by his mother, his father and society. He has shaved his head and mutilated himself in many ways.

Matt has been too scared to come back to Ardoch for a long time. He came to enrol at Prahran because Mike and I were there. The first thing Matt did when he saw me on the first day of school was rush up and give me a big hug.

I am delighted that in the first month of the 1993 school year we have put on two more flats in response to the expanded need at Prahran.

I feel that our work over the past five years has been significant in a societal sense in that we have been representing all homeless and at risk students.

4

Communities Working Together

Supporting the Ardoch Programs

John Bell, Managing Director, Esprit

It is something we wanted to do. My understanding of social justice is a home, an education and a job. Kathy Hilton has some sort of structure there that we can work with. It was a way to do a pilot and we have used the pilot to help other kids.

We support four kids at Ardoch and the staff get involved. We have very good accommodation and employment programs running. We also have a farm where we have kids from prison.

I think I can be a role model for other business people. You have to set a good example. I feel I am part of changing society's attitudes to youth homelessness. We have set up an organisation, Business and Community for Young People. The idea of the organisation is to encourage other business people to employ or educate a young person.

My focus now is duplicating what we are doing. There is no excuse for people saying they don't know what to do to help. There are not enough Kathy Hiltons in the world. We have to get more people in the community doing their share.

Barbara Black, teacher, Mount Scopus Memorial College

We established a liaison with Ardoch in 1988 and each year Ardoch students visit year 11 at Mount Scopus. The first time Kathy and the Ardoch students spoke at the school it really mobilised our kids to action. The Ardoch kids were very powerful and gave our kids a new perspective. The Mount Scopus kids were stunned as they had never heard anything like it in their lives. They wanted to do something to help to be involved, not just give money.

One of the girls from Ardoch who came to speak in the first year developed a friendship with a Mount Scopus student and they are now at university together.

The second year the Ardoch students came to the school, we provided lunch so that the kids could mix together. The Scopus kids bought food and toiletries for the Ardoch kids and donated money.

We kept our involvement low key because we didn't want to exploit the situation. Whatever the Scopus kids have done for Ardoch, they have done themselves.

I think it would be good if there was more communication between the Scopus kids and the Ardoch kids.

I have asked Scopus kids about where the responsibility lies for homeless kids. They responded that we are all responsible. In the long run, I hope they will internalise this. I hope when our kids leave school they will be much more caring people.

Tony Conabere, Principal, Wesley College

In 1989 I read about what Kathy Hilton was doing at Ardoch and I felt we should be supporting it. I was impressed with the practical things Kathy was doing.

Kathy and several homeless students from Ardoch came and spoke at Wesley. It was certainly one of the most significant days in the careers of 450 students at Wesley. The effect on the school was quite electrifying. The staff and students came from such a base of privilege that they had never really seen youth homelessness. We are all cocooned quite nicely.

As Kathy and the Ardoch students spoke, the Wesley audience realised that some young people are dealt a very bad deal. The atmosphere was amazing. The applause at the end was over the top. Immediately, charities at the school for that year were dominated by Ardoch.

I can still hear Kathy saying that there are 500 homeless children sleeping on the streets within 3 kilometres of Wesley. So it is our problem.

Kathy's daughter was in year 10 at Wesley and her group of friends suggested that Wesley should finance one flat each year. We committed to financing a flat plus doing other things when we had extra money.

In 1991 Kathy came to Wesley again to speak to the Purple and Gold Committee. Eloise also came to talk and members of the committee met a charming, eloquent and successful university student. Committee members also committed to assisting Ardoch. For example, they have furnished one of the flats.

The Purple and Gold Committee took it a step further and invited representatives from all the independent schools to a meeting to hear Kathy. As a result, a very large function will be held in 1993 to raise funds for Ardoch. They are hoping to raise $25 000.

I think the student support program developed at Ardoch has so much to say to the community about the fact that these kids need another chance, that they will take another chance. The program is giving the homeless kids a lot of skills and the kids have to work hard.

By the end of 1992 we had raised approximately $30 000 for Ardoch. The student support program is very high on our priorities. We feel that the money we give is going in a really good direction because we know what the program can achieve.

The Wesley kids were touched by Kathy and the homeless kids from Ardoch because it was their own talking to them. They are all part of the same community, they listen to the same music. There was empathy.

I admire Kathy and the people who are supporting her because they are actually doing something. They are acting on their concern for homeless students.

I am contributing to the Ardoch Youth Foundation because the pressure has to be taken off Kathy so that she can get on with her job of dealing with the kids. We need to extend the support structures for Kathy and let her go on developing the program at Prahran Secondary College. It is important that Kathy doesn't lose contact with the homeless kids.

Kathy has a fantastic commitment to the kids and a sense of faith in them. She has a feeling for the humanity of each student. She has given the homeless kids a sense that there is a future, that they can participate if they want to and that society hasn't absolutely rejected them. Kathy has also made the kids face up to the fact that if they are going to make it they have to do it on society's terms, not their own terms. She has given them faith in themselves.

The wonderful thing about the student support program is that it is bringing people together from the school community and the broader community. The needs of the homeless kids are being met in a very special way under very difficult circumstances.

Trish Bainbridge, Genazzano Community Support Group

Kathy Hilton spoke to the Genazzano girls in 1991 and they subsequently collected toiletries for the Ardoch students.

In 1992 Genazzano FCJ College had a year 12 social awareness night and Kathy Hilton was one of the speakers on the subject of poverty and street kids. I went along as an interested parent. Kathy touched me so much that at the annual general meeting of the Genazzano parents' support group I suggested that we did something for the kids at Ardoch.

Margaret Hill and I organised for the Genazzano mums to put on a lunch for all the kids at Ardoch once a term. It is a special lunch on the last day of term. The mothers provide all the food and a catering firm in Richmond provides the cutlery and crockery.

I think the mothers make a contribution to Ardoch because they have got kids the same age who are in a different situation to the kids at Ardoch. We have got a large resource in the mothers who have the skills to support the program at Ardoch. The Ardoch students think it is wonderful food.

I think this style of support fits in with the philosophy and environment at Ardoch. At the first lunch one of the kids said this is wonderful; everyone in the school cares about us. We at Genazzano want to be part of that whole caring school.

The Parents' Association has again voted for part of the proceeds of the school fair to go to Ardoch.

The girls at Genazzano are now aware of Ardoch. They talk about the homeless kids and influence their parents about the importance of helping Ardoch.

I can honestly say that before I heard Kathy, I hadn't really thought about what our society could do for homeless kids. I personally want to do more. In fact this morning, I got a copy of the Liberal Party Street Kids Policy which is something I have not done in my life before.

I am sure the Genazzano effort is a help financially. I hope by our support we also encourage the administration part of the program at Ardoch. I also think we can go into the general community for Ardoch.

We are very pleased with the response we in turn have received from the Ardoch kids.

Vaughn Clare, Director, Readydata

I was really looking for a community project so that I could put something back into the community. I heard about Ardoch through Streetgang, a community-based organisation formed to help street kids. At that stage there was a funding crisis at Ardoch. I joined with a group of colleagues in raising $1 300 to keep the program going for a week.

I went to Ardoch to find out more about the program and was taken aback when Kathy explained that there was no real funding structure in place to support the work at the school. We recognised that a legal structure with tax deductibility would be important for raising money to support the program. We set up the Ardoch Youth Foundation.

Kathy Hilton has been inspiring to a lot of people with her vision for the program. She made a difference to keeping me involved and keeping me inspired.

I think persistence is the most valuable skill I have brought to the program. My business acumen has helped in setting up the foundation.

The breakfast program for the kids at Ardoch was something that Kathy and Mike had been wanting to implement at the school. I feel quite proud that I was part of getting the breakfast program going. Attending the breakfast program continually inspires me.

The breakfast program is one of the most significant things at Ardoch because of the way it brings a wide variety people in and gets them involved. It is a lot more than just a meal in the morning.

In the beginning the kids were insular and there wasn't a lot of communication. When Graeme Wise from The Body Shop got involved—it made a difference. It meant there were people there for the kids on a constant basis. The atmosphere has been building ever since. Now there is lots of laughing and talking.

I think my main task now is getting the foundation going. I am more a background person. I am good at getting things done, planning and implementing.

Since being involved with Ardoch I have realised what a lot of potential there is in these kids. Ardoch can help to bring that potential out.

The next step is to use the experience of Ardoch to set up a program in other schools. It is also important to change the philosophy of what schools are about. I think that is an important function of the foundation. The program has to be bigger than one school.

The successes like Eloise are the highlight of the program. Her development over the past few years is an inspiration to me.

Julie Rothbart, parent

Initially I was a primary school teacher. I love kids. When I heard that Ardoch wanted to start a breakfast program, I said I would love to help. I have been going every day since the program started, arriving at 7.00 a.m.

I see myself as a constant factor which is important because many of the kids don't have that in their lives.

The whole atmosphere in the breakfast program has changed over time. Kids who had nothing to look forward to at school come in smiling. Now they help with the washing up, they help each other, they talk to each other and they say thanks for the breakfast.

The teachers have advised that since the breakfast program started, the kids are much calmer in the classroom and much more responsive. It is a combination of the food, the people who come every day, the caring, and the nurturing. You can see them blossoming like flowers.

During conversation with the kids I encourage them to aim higher. I have no expectations of the kids. I accept them as they are.

I approached one of the big supermarket chains and there was so much red tape to get any donation of food. My local greengrocer, supermarket and bread shop have been wonderful giving us food.

I encourage the kids to make lunch and a snack for later while they are at the breakfast program. Some of them ask for food to take home and I pack a bag for them.

In the first few weeks, it took time to bring them into the room. I used to cook sausages outside to entice them in with the smell. They have a lot of pride which is great. Once the kids come to the breakfast program, they become regulars.

This breakfast program could happen in any community in Australia. It is just finding people who love kids and care about their welfare.

It is important that the volunteers who are rostered on don't try and impose their values on the kids. Our role is to be there for the kids and to provide nourishment.

We try to treat the kids like individuals, to make them feel special and that somebody really cares. For example, one boy had an arm operation and I visited him in hospital. I took fruit and his favourite cake. He calls me mum.

Once a month, we have a birthday cake for all the kids whose birthday falls in that month. We sing 'Happy Birthday'. A lot of those kids haven't seen a birthday cake for a long time.

To help the kids manage the holidays we try to provide them with food that they can eat over that period. Unfortunately, the school is not open during the holidays.

I have watched the kids develop a sense of respect for the breakfast program room. If something was spilt they used to leave it, now they clean it up.

Commitment and Support

Graeme Wise, Director, The Body Shop

The Body Shop has always had a philosophy that business should put back into the community. Every shop in the organisation has a community project. One of our staff suggested we should help Ardoch. It started off in a very small way, just collecting donations.

When I got to the breakfast program, I felt that this was an important thing to do so I participated as often as I could, generally three times a week.

I felt that one of the main needs of the kids at the breakfast program was the continuity of contact with adults. It was an opportunity for me to get to know the kids and to develop a mentor relationship with them. I knew I had to earn their trust and get them to understand that I wasn't a fly-by-night.

I have tried to build a relationship with the kids so that they can turn to me for advice. I go to sit and talk to the kids and it is getting easier every day. I get a lot of enjoyment from being involved with the kids at Ardoch. It is an important part of my life now.

There is a family atmosphere being created at the breakfast program and I like to feel that I am part of that atmosphere. The staff from The Body Shop are also becoming accepted.

Most people like to belong to an organisation that cares about other people. We encourage staff to think about other people. Long term, we would like to involve our customers in these types of positive community projects.

I feel very proud of what Ardoch is doing.

The crucial thing about the program at Ardoch is that it is only a small group of people participating. I would like to see the Ardoch concept adopted throughout the whole country. It is a shame that some of the kids are coming long distances because there aren't any schools in other areas that address the needs of homeless and at-risk students.

I think schools need to look at their role as a community role, not just an education role.

I think business in general has so much to gain from getting involved in something like the support program at Ardoch. The involvement with helping others motivates staff and it does reflect on your company.

What really gives us a lot of joy is the number of people in the whole organisation that think that the program at Ardoch is something special. Recently the guys at the warehouse used the company van on a Saturday to move two of the Ardoch students from one flat to another.

My partner and I, through the company's resources, fund two flats and guarantee the lease on a house. That is something we can do with money. There are a lot of things we do for the program which only cost time and commitment. Anyone can do those things.

Leah Black, Shalom Unit, B'nai B'rith

The Shalom Unit of the B'nai B'rith, a community services organisation, supports Ardoch. I am chairman of the Shalom Services Committee.

For two years one of our projects has been to raise funds to buy groceries and toiletries for the children at Ardoch. We give money boxes to members at our monthly meetings. When they bring in the money collected, I go shopping and buy the goods.

We also collect clothing and furniture for the kids at Ardoch. I go through the clothing first to make sure it is suitable for the young people.

We had a sweet stall at the end of 1992 and a proportion of the money raised from that went to Ardoch.

We heard about Ardoch from a member who knows Kathy Hilton. Kathy came to one of my meetings with two Ardoch students to talk to the members. That's when our members decided to help the kids at Ardoch. We have about 150 members.

Tania Grundfeld, University Student

My first exposure to homeless kids was when I was in year 11 and the Ardoch kids came to my school. I was quite shocked. Even though I had heard about youth homelessness through my auntie, I really didn't understand until I met the kids. I was quite surprised to see that they were normal kids like me.

Going to a private school, I had not been exposed to youth homelessness. I had always associated homelessness with America. I now realise that some parents don't care about their children. I was raised in a very caring family.

Eloise was one of the kids who came to my school and we have become friends. She worked with me in my father's factory over the school holidays. We were cutting up vegetables. It gave me an opportunity to get to know Eloise very well.

I am studying at university and my direction is to be a psychologist. I feel I will devote some of my time to helping people who are not very well off.

I have informally raised awareness about youth homelessness among friends and acquaintances. I found that there was a lot of ignorance.

Last Passover I tried to collect all the wheat products from Jewish homes in my area to give to Ardoch. I often got questions like, 'Are there homeless people in Australia?'

The feeling among my peer group about young homeless people is generally pity. I don't think they give it much thought unfortunately. Often they just think they are drop-out kids that want a bit of freedom. The stereotype is that the homeless kids are on drugs and that their situation is their own fault.

I have a problem with the fact that the homeless kids are often afraid of other kids. There tends to be a lack of trust. I would like to see the homeless kids mixing more with their peers from other situations. It is almost unhealthy that most of their social activities are with other homeless kids.

I remember Eloise found it very depressing that as she was getting out of her situation she was surrounded by people who would often pull her down. She was afraid that she would regress. I wish a project could be developed to encourage homeless kids to mix with kids from all areas of society.

Sasha Wood-Bradley, Firbank Anglican School

The homeless kids from Ardoch came to Firbank at the end of 1992. What they said made me feel selfish. I realised that I take everything from my parents for granted. The way the support program has been set up with only a bit of help from the government is incredible.

Firbank students want to help fund a flat and we will continue to support Ardoch students through various fund-raising activities. I think that would be more productive than the way we donate small amounts to different charities. I think it would be more beneficial in the long run to educate and support children our own age.

I didn't know what youth homelessness was until the kids from Ardoch came to talk to us. I am a little informed but there is a lot more I feel I should know.

I think it must have taken a lot for the Ardoch kids to come and talk to a highly financial and privileged school. It would take courage and incredible determination to get out and show what can be done to help homeless kids.

Katherine Evans, Firbank Anglican School

I had heard a lot about the homeless problem from Eloise, the first homeless student at Ardoch. Eloise was a student teacher at Firbank in 1992 and for about six lessons we talked about the issue of homelessness and Ardoch.

When the kids from Ardoch were speaking, I felt sympathetic but I wanted to feel more empathetic. Also I felt frustrated that I wasn't helping, that I was taking things for granted.

I feel determined to help the homeless kids in some way. I would like our school to set up a flat. I am sure we would be able to do something like that. Very likely I will help to make this happen. I think my whole class will try and do something to help the problem.

Ruth Webster, Retired

I read about the program at Ardoch in the newspaper and I was very impressed with Kathy Hilton. I decided to do what I could to help. I collected clothing and kitchen utensils and bought food for the young people. I get the clothing from some young wealthy friends. I stick to that because there is not much I can do. I had a stroke.

I have met some of the girls from Ardoch and I am very impressed.

I feel the more that people know about the program the better. I am most definitely spreading the word about Ardoch. I feel fortunate that I can help the kids.

It is quite remarkable that Kathy cares so much about the kids. She is there for the kids and I think they love her.

I have only recently become aware of sexual abuse in families. This wasn't talked about years ago.

The program at Ardoch makes the kids feel that someone cares about them.

The important thing is that the kids want to make something of themselves.

Jenny Grey, Counsellor, Prahran Community Health Centre

In my counselling work at the school, I was certainly seeing far more abuse in recent years. I visited Ardoch on a weekly basis over the last decade.

The youth homeless program slowly emerged and then it hotted up as more homeless children attended the school. There were also a lot of other children at the school who were living at home but in difficult circumstances.

I think the support should be there for young people who have the motivation and drive to return to school and improve themselves.

The program that Kathy has instituted is an excellent program. However it is a shame that there is not more support from government. Ardoch-Windsor Secondary College should also be recognised as a special needs school and staffed accordingly.

Basically what I would like to see is the school staffed properly by the education department and a committee of people from the community who can assist with the planning. There needs to be a program that has proper resources so that these young people are properly helped rather than a band-aid approach.

One of the crucial things is that the kids at Ardoch are not sent away from the school for counselling services. The school is seen by the kids as a safe place.

If we don't intervene, the kids' problems are going to go on for ever. The school is the best place for intervention. Some of the kids keep dropping out of school and often it is because they are not getting the support they require. Sometimes kids drop out because their lives are too damaged. For these kids intervention should have happened a lot earlier.

It is horrific that there are government ministries that don't talk across ministries. The money spent by the different ministries could be put into something worthwhile.

Someone like Kathy is needed in the support program to give the kids the feeling that someone cares about them. However, they also need the other services too.

I am a person to help the kids facilitate change and to help them learn skills. The aim is for them to take responsibility for their own actions, for them to be able to choose and to realise that they have rights. I help them develop their self esteem. Some of the kids continue to see me when they move on to university.

Dr Alex Starr, Dental Surgeon

I feel as a health professional that it is vitally important to help disadvantaged young people like street kids so that, apart from alleviating any dental problems, they feel that they are not being forgotten by society. In general their dental care has been neglected for a long period of time.

I treat the homeless kids in my busy practice in the same way that I treat my paying patients. I find that there is a natural reaction of gratitude from the kids because they are being treated the same as other people. I think this helps with their self-esteem and makes them feel that other people really care about them.

One of the homeless students had an accident and damaged her teeth. After I treated the pain and repaired the broken teeth she expressed her joy at being able to smile again. The feedback I get from the homeless kids has been very rewarding.

There appears to be a growing need to help homeless young people with dental health care.

Denis Muller, Education Editor, *Age*

On the first day of the 1993 school year, I visited the Prahran Secondary College to see what had happened to the homeless kids of Ardoch-Windsor. I found Russell Harrison, the principal, energetically positive about having the Ardoch kids, and their support staff. He readily agreed to let me talk to Kathy Hilton.

We found her in the library surrounded by kids who needed—well, everything. But especially they seemed to need her.

Up close she was such a surprise. I had expected to find a highly politicised sort of dungaree activist with plenty of spleen to vent against the state government. What I found was a radiantly warm person who spoke of how she loved these kids, how she had begun to help them. She spoke of her philosophy: how the program was all about self-help, personal choices and individual responsibility.

In the space of an hour, I watched her handle one small crisis after another always giving of herself—hugging, smiling, comforting, advising. Where did she get this strength, this generosity? She was inspirational.

That afternoon I was talking to a group of senior people from the independent schools. They were saying how many good things happened in schools but never got reported. I told them about Kathy Hilton and Prahran Secondary College. Here is the story I wrote.

> It is half past-seven on a warm drizzly morning, the first week back at school. Under the concrete canopy of an austere piece of modern architecture, 50 or 60 kids are gathered in small knots. Some are sitting on the ground or slatted wooden benches. Others stand around a bulky stainless steel barbecue machine awash in spitting sausages.
>
> The occasion is breakfast, but something more: a kind of reaching out by the students displaced at the end of last year from Ardoch-Windsor Secondary College, to their fellow students at Prahran Secondary, where they have made their new home.
>
> When it had been announced late last year that Ardoch-Windsor would be closed as part of the cuts in

education spending, there was widespread concern that its program for more than 100 homeless and disadvantaged students would evaporate. Would their lifeline to a secure future die with the school?

It didn't. Over the summer holidays the Education Ministry gave them a tumbledown weatherboard house in a narrow street beside Prahran Secondary. Basic repairs were made and the kids painted the interior. It has a pantry from which they can take food, a bathroom and a laundry.

When school resumed nearly all the kids from last year turned up. The principal, Mr Russell Harrison, made a speech of welcome—not just to Ardoch kids but to the 40 per cent of his entire student body beginning at Prahran that day. Breakfast was supplied, as had been the practice at Ardoch-Windsor, for anyone who needed it, lunch too.

Most importantly Kathy Hilton was there. Russell Harrison sought her out in the library. She was lost among a group of young men and women gathered around her for support.

Kathy Hilton occupies a place in the lives of these young people that goes far beyond her formal position of English teacher and welfare co-ordinator. She is someone around whom they are rebuilding their lives.

Eloise was four when her family disintegrated. Her mother and father split. Her relatives were scattered across the continent.

By the time she was 12 she had run away several times; at the end of year 10 she left school. 'I felt I had to become independent.' This meant being able to earn money. She began a hair dressing apprenticeship and took odd jobs to supplement her wage. By now she was supporting her brother as well. He was 12. They got a flat but the rent made too much of a hole in her budget. 'We were not able to buy enough food to survive.'

She boarded with friends, then it was squats. When the squats were purged, she was on the streets. After two years of the street scene with its drugs, violence and betrayal, she wanted out. 'I decided to go back to school, because I saw that as a way out of the poverty trap I was caught in.'

It was 1988. The school was Ardoch High School, which became Ardoch-Windsor Secondary.

Academically she did well, but the poverty was grinding her down. There was no AUSTUDY, she didn't have enough cash for rent and her nomadic existence was making schooling impossible. Some days she was put in the sick bay to get some sleep.

Her prize possession was a waist-length leather jacket which doubled as clothing and collateral. When she ran out of money she pawned it.

In about September that year she went to Kathy Hilton for help. 'I'd had enough of not having enough money to even be able to eat properly. I'd live on potatoes and two minute noodles. I was physically starving. I just wanted somewhere to live, somewhere safe, where I could get on with my education.'

Kathy Hilton listened while Eloise told her the story of her life. 'I was shocked I didn't know what to do. But I didn't say come back when you've got a house, or when you've got money for books or when you've had your dental work done or when you've got a tram ticket, or when you've got food.'

Instead, she made an innocent assumption that there were experts to cope with this. She spent her lunchtime on the phone. No fewer than seven government agencies identified themselves as having some responsibility: none had a pigeon hole that quite fitted the case.

She found Eloise a room in a hostel, provided her with furniture and clothing, bought her reading glasses.

'By the next year, the word went around, and the whole house where Eloise was eventually placed, came to school.'

Ardoch suddenly had 12 kids like Eloise—destitute but determined to use education as their ticket out of poverty.

'We went to the ministry—Mrs Kirner was the Minister for Education—and we got a good hearing. But political pipelines are so long and you can't tell a kid to wait 18 months for a roof over his head.'

Ardoch responded on two levels: providing the kids with their immediate needs (like food, toothbrushes and toiletries) and raising community awareness. By the third year there were 38 kids to look after. It was getting too much for one person.

As it happened Ardoch was doing the right thing at the right time. The Burdekin Report on homeless youth had generated the 'Students At Risk' Program and the bureaucracy was now looking for ways of implementing it. The school was granted $18 000 a year, enough to employ a youth worker as part of a pilot program. It's still going.

At the same time, all the assistance with housing, food, clothing, medical services and the rest continue to be provided from voluntary sources. Last year, Ardoch-Windsor raised $150 000 for this work.

At the end of 1989, Eloise passed her HSC.

She was accepted into Melbourne University and embarked on a bachelor of Arts degree majoring in education. Three others from Ardoch's year of '89 got into uni as well. A couple of years later her brother got in too.

Academically she brought to her sociology course a solid grounding in the real world.

This is her fourth and final year. The iron determination that has borne her off the streets, through high school and university is also the raw material out of which she has fashioned a sharp-edged ambition to change the world. 'What I really want to do is be part of empowering people, part of making a change in this world for young people.'

She is a role model for her peers, and reinforces Kathy Hilton's philosophy that the Ardoch culture is nothing to do with charity and everything to do with self-help.

She is vice-president of the Ardoch Foundation, a grand-sounding body which Kathy Hilton, as president, insists is far from grand. Its purpose is to raise money to continue the work.

A mohawk haircut appears, announcing the presence of Marcus. He is a tall, pale, wiry youth with a stud in his nose, a glitter in his eye and, on his feet, two basketball shoes—possibly a pair one sprayed yellow and the other black. Never having had shoes bought for him, he doesn't know what size he takes.

Marcus is agitated. He proclaims that he has just told Russell Harrison to get stuffed, although further investigation proves this to be bravado. Kathy Hilton draws him to her and reaches up to put her arms around his neck. He holds himself to her for a moment while she quietly reproaches him for the futility of telling anyone to get stuffed, any time.

It is day one at Prahran, and a tense occasion. Kathy Hilton is anxious. 'They are all scared. But we promised we would stick together and we have.'

This feature article was published in the *Age* on 1 March 1993.

5

The Role of Schools: Learning from the Ardoch Experience

Raising Awareness of the Issues

Any review of the Ardoch student support program must begin with the question of awareness. Prior to 1988 none of the people currently associated with the program, whether principal, teacher or supporter from the broader community, was aware of the extent of youth homelessness, the depth of the plight of homeless children or the range of their needs. The Burdekin Report has put the problems of homeless youths and children firmly on the political agenda and has helped to raise awareness in the community. It is clear, however, that there are still teachers and educationalists who have not read the report itself, nor any summary of it nor other material on homelessness. It is also likely that there are schools, teachers and educationalists who have not absorbed the lessons of Burdekin that schools have consistently failed homeless children, that homeless children face special problems in school and that they have even more difficult problems of re-entry into the educational system when they have dropped out.

Not every school will or necessarily should be equipped to look after significant numbers of homeless children; there is an important argument for developing extensive programs in a limited number of schools which will be discussed later in this chapter. However, every principal and every teacher should be given some training in issues related to homeless and at-risk young people. Often no more may be required than understanding and empathy for the likely problems faced by homeless young people, willingness to help find suitable assistance and some knowledge of where to turn to. Schools and teachers especially need to understand that because many homeless students have been seriously neglected, exploited or abused (virtually all the young people interviewed for this book are in this category), most suffer from serious lack of self-esteem and most are very wary of societal institutions (including schools). Some may have also learnt coping behaviours which can be anti-social or disruptive.

If this awareness can be generated, and together with it some simple rules for the identification and handling of homeless young people, then the first problem identified in the Burdekin Report, that is, the role that schools play in contributing to homelessness, can be overcome.

Dispelling the Myths

There are many prevailing myths and assumptions about youth homelessness. A key part of awareness generation must be concerned with the dispelling of these myths. The Burdekin Report addressed the myths that most children leave home of their own accord and that homelessness is a life of freedom for children. As the Ardoch experience illustrates, young people leave home for a variety of reasons. Most, however, leave in response to poverty, neglect or repetitive abuse. 'Sometimes the home leaves the kids.' The Burdekin investigations and the Ardoch experience also show that homelessness is a life of powerlessness, poverty and often abuse.

The Ardoch support program has shown that the assumption that the problem of youth homelessness is too big and that nothing can be done about it is false. It has demonstrated that homelessness does not have to lead inevitably to school dropout. It has shown that many homeless young people would choose to be at school if it was made a real option—that is, if the necessary support was made available. It has demonstrated what can be done if the education system is flexible enough and the support available. It has shown that there are many people who want to help homeless young people. The program has also illustrated the importance of partnerships between schools, government agencies and members of the community. It has clearly shown that homelessness is not a problem to be left to government alone but requires the involvement of people in many different spheres of activity. Publicity about the program has played an important part in the dispelling of these many myths.

The Potential of the School System

The authors of the Burdekin Report seem to have concentrated their main attention on identifying and removing the negative influence of schools. The Ardoch experience tells us that schools are also in a special position to help homeless students. A next step, therefore, is that all those involved in the educational system and all those concerned with housing and welfare support for homeless young people come to recognise the potential of the school system. Earlier in this book we have argued that the school was the one stable and potentially neutral institution within which all homeless children spend some time, that education is the primary route for young people to escape poverty, and that the school provides an environment in which homeless children can meet and associate with their peers, those who are experiencing similar problems as much as those who come from more stable environments. There is a real need to listen to young people. The school is an ideal place to listen, hear and find out what the problems really are. The school can, for example, be a place where problems such as access to income support, appropriate housing, therapy needs can be identified and steps taken to deal with them. The Ardoch experience shows that schools can play all these roles and provide all these different forms of support. If, and only if, this potential is widely recognised can the school system start to respond in a more effective way.

Essential Ingredients for a Student Support Program

Based on the Ardoch experience and information on other school based initiatives, what are the essential ingredients for an effective school program? First, there must be a supportive environment in the school. The school must welcome children irrespective of their backgrounds and must not stigmatise those who come with homeless experiences and who may as a consequence have learning difficulties or behavioural problems. The atmosphere must be generated and led from the top and fully accepted throughout the school. There must be very skilled and caring people available to have the primary contact with homeless and at-risk young people. This support service needs to be available to all young people including mature-age students and part-time students.

The Ardoch experience suggests that it is helpful for homeless young people to be associated with others who share their problems as well as with members of their wider peer group. It seems clear, from the experience of those interviewed by O'Connor for the National Inquiry Into Homeless Children and of those interviewed as part of the research for this book, that homeless children have as many problems with their peers as with teachers and school authorities. If homeless children are to be retained in school or attracted back into school they must feel not only that the school and the teachers will be sympathetic and supportive but also that their fellow students will not label, denigrate or look down on them. Thus, the overall atmosphere in the school, that created by the teachers and authorities and that created by the students, must be natural, relaxed and very supportive.

Another critical lesson from Ardoch is that no homeless child can be expected to remain at school and to perform at even the minimal level of competency unless his or her basic physical needs are being looked after. The lunch and breakfast programs and the school pantry at Ardoch developed to meet this need. No program for homeless students will succeed unless it includes such measures to feed children who are chronically undernourished and sometimes starving.

The Ardoch breakfast program has served another very important purpose. It has provided a warm and comfortable environment for homeless and underprivileged young people. It gives them easy contact with people from many different walks of life and with other young people of similar backgrounds, many of whom are beginning the difficult journey of re-entry into the school and are learning to rid themselves of debilitating habits and addictions. It gives them another way of interacting with their peers and adults from the broader community. It is an act of giving; it asks nothing of the students. It is thus a way not only of giving the children the basic means of survival but also of breaking down the distrust, suspicion and cynicism with which homeless children tend to treat all adults and institutions.

Young people cannot cope with school, neither the work nor the interaction with teachers nor the relationships with their peers, unless they have an adequate home. The examples cited in the O'Connor research, some of which were recorded in chapter 1, make this abundantly clear. As Kathy Hilton and others have explained, Ardoch found itself drawn directly into the task of finding accommodation for its homeless students. With a program like that at Ardoch, the caring people involved are in a position to identify needs clearly. A young person may have shelter but this may prove to be inappropriate and unsatisfactory. Eloise, for example, was sent to a house with a drug pusher and unemployed women who partied all night. Kathy has spoken of the 'horrifying' nature of some of the emergency housing that had been available and the way that the kids avoided this kind of housing if they could.

People involved in the Ardoch program have played a very important role in finding more suitable emergency accommodation, sometimes offering it themselves. They have worked with other agencies to find longer term accommodation. Outside groups, in this instance The Body Shop, Esprit and Wesley College, have helped to provide safe housing.

Support from the Broader Community

Community support for the Ardoch initiative has been crucially important. Without it there would be no breakfast program, no direct rental assistance, and no Ardoch flats and inadequate dental, optical and health support. Not the least of the contributions of the outside helpers has been to provide contact for homeless kids with a supportive adult world, an experience they may never have previously had. Those coming in from the wider community have also been able to give those working in the school other kinds of help and encouragement. Working with homeless children makes heavy demands on the people concerned. Mostly it is a long-term process. The young people have often had very painful experiences and carry the scars of those experiences. Most 'take two steps forwards and one step back'. Many are not used to having choices of any kind. With the choices they are offered come responsibility; learning to take responsibility for their own actions can be difficult and taxing. To dedicated staff there are the rewards of successful rehabilitation. But together with those successes there are also children who cannot cope and slip back into their old habits. Often the children take out their frustrations on those who are working hardest for them. The moral and personal support that committed people from the outside community can give to those who are working daily with these problems is thus of the greatest possible significance.

The Role of Government

There is a need for a significant change in attitude to take place in schools and in government and community agencies. Grass roots experience needs to be fed back into policy and seen as constructive comment; greater value needs to be given to first hand experience. Government agencies need to recognise that the problems of homeless youths often require immediate responses. Those working in the field feel strongly that government programs take too long to develop and by the time they are developed, they are sometimes inappropriate.

A critical problem appears to be the lack of information about youth homelessness in the education system. If a serious attempt is to be made to keep homeless young people in schools and to use the school system, there needs to be a more effective and systematic means of collecting information. This is an essential step. A requirement placed on schools to collect information might also greatly help to raise awareness of and sensitivity towards homeless children and their problems. Adequate resources would, however, need to be provided to co-ordinate and disseminate this information.

There also needs to be more effective co-ordination between government agencies. The frustrations of being referred from one agency to another is tellingly expressed by those in the Ardoch program.

Prevention

Government policy and school programs should concentrate as much as possible on prevention. Leaving aside the evident benefits to the young people concerned, prevention could save the community untold expense as Daryl Dixon cogently argues in chapter 8. Schools are the obvious place in which to concentrate. Homelessness is usually the end result of stress and abuse. During this build up of pressure on the young people concerned, the school is one of the few places, if not the only place, where it might be observed and identified. An important part of the Ardoch program has been its emphasis on preventative measures for those at risk of becoming homeless.

Ideally there should be at least one person in every school trained as a student welfare co-ordinator to identify and deal with homeless and at risk students. Such a person could handle referrals from other members of staff, liaise with other support agencies and co-ordinate community help. The student welfare co-ordinator's role should be given status and priority and student welfare co-ordinators should be properly trained.

Some Cautions

The Ardoch experience provides a remarkable example of a school program which has dealt with all the multi-faceted dimensions of homelessness and found answers for very many of them. It has assembled and retained in the school system a large number of homeless students, testimony in itself to the success of the program given the inexorable pattern of school drop-out which characterises the experience of homeless young people.

It would be absurd to suggest that the Ardoch program can be established in every school of Australia. The Burdekin Report (Human Rights and Equal Opportunity Commission 1989: 278) quoted a passage in the 1988 report prepared by the Princeton based Carnegie Foundation for the Advancement of Teaching. This report followed surveys of 22 000 teachers across the USA. The passage is worth repeating in full:

> In an odd way this report isn't about teaching, it's about the extent to which the schools have been made to stand in for

providers of everything from child nutrition and family life to socialisation and values. This is a familiar complaint and a vague one; here it is put into numbers. Ninety per cent of teachers nation-wide cite 'lack of parental support' for their efforts; eighty-nine per cent say they see abused or neglected children, sixty-eight per cent say that undernourishment is a problem at their school, 69% poor health ... Even a few children in these kinds of distress constitute a considerable burden on the teacher. That doesn't say much for the likelihood of an abused, ill, hungry or an even ordinary child getting enough help at school to counter a bad home situation. Those reposing their hopes in the schools and in the teachers as the best place to attack these problems had better start giving those all important players the resources and support they deserve.

Many schools and teachers feel that their responsibility is to educate children in the school environment and that they cannot reasonably be asked to carry the full burden of caring for children who have been abandoned by their families and society, nor for the children who have serious problems at home. Many feel that, were they to attempt to play these additional roles, it would be at the expense of their other teaching responsibilities. Most would feel that they were quite ill-equipped to help.

Although the Ardoch program has shown that there are people who are willing to help when they understand the problem and the opportunity is presented to them, it would nevertheless be very difficult to find committed people like those mentioned in this book to put together a very large number of programs and activities similar to the Ardoch student-support program. If it were not so, these programs would be found all over Australia and *Our Homeless Children*, the Human Rights and Equal Opportunity Commission report, might have had a very different message.

The first need, therefore, is that existing programs like that at Ardoch are given all the support they need to continue to function. Within such schools there is likely to be a need for more flexibility in curricula and other approaches since they are not always appropriate for homeless and at-risk students. More

Housing Support
Students from Prahran Secondary College in their home which is
sponsored by Esprit and The Body Shop

All photographs by Carlos Alcaide

Volunteer Support from the Broader Community
Prahran Secondary College students at the breakfast program with a volunteer, Debbie Wyatt looking at her daughter Ashley

Support from School Staff and the Ardoch Youth Foundation
(*Left to right*) Vaughn Clare, Russell Harrison, Kathy Hilton, Graeme Wise and Eloise Tregonning (*seated*) with Prahran Secondary College students at the breakfast program

Ardoch Graduate now in a Teaching Role
Eloise Tregonning (*second from right*) in the school library with a Prahran Secondary College student and Wesley College students

Sharing Environment
A Prahran Secondary College student enjoying breakfast at the breakfast program with a Wesley College student

Julie Rothbart serving food to Prahran Secondary College students at the breakfast program

qualified youth workers are needed for outreach work. Continuity for young people is also very important.

New programs based on the Ardoch support program should be encouraged, developed and supported in some selected schools. Such schools must be willing to cater for students whatever their background and to treat all those students as equal whatever their learning difficulties or outside circumstances. The schools need principals and staff who want to look after homeless young people and have a commitment to them. They need dedicated individuals who have the appropriate skills, training and personal involvement. They need considerable support from outside agencies. They also need committed members of the broader community to provide concrete and moral support.

In all other schools, as we have argued, it is important to raise the level of awareness so that homelessness and all the associated problems can be more quickly identified and dealt with.

The Urgency

We finally need to be reminded of the dimensions of homelessness in Australia, issues that are more fully explored in the following chapters. The Ardoch program and other similar initiatives are inspiring examples but are reaching a pitifully small percentage of homeless children. This is no fault of or reflection on them. It is extraordinary that Ardoch and Prahran Secondary Colleges have even retained the homeless and at-risk children who have enrolled with them. What we know about youth homelessness, however, suggests that the Ardoch support program and the other programs cited in chapter 1 have been dealing with no more 5 or 6 per cent of homeless young people in Melbourne. This figure furthermore takes no account of the many students currently at risk of becoming homeless. This is a sobering measure of the urgency with which we need to act.

Part Two

6

The Dilemmas of Youth Homelessness

In the first part of the book some remarkable examples are given of the way schools can support homeless young people. As the last chapter concludes, however, these are isolated examples of individual initiatives and not representative of the education system as a whole. Furthermore, these programs are only supporting a small percentage of homeless young people.

A systematic approach to the problems of youth homelessness needs to begin with the exploration and analysis of the underlying elements. The first step is to estimate the likely number of homeless young people in order to establish the dimensions of the problem. This chapter therefore begins with a discussion about estimates. It then examines possible causes of youth homelessness. An important theme is that the nature of the conclusions reached about the causes of youth homelessness will strongly influence the likely policy responses.

Estimating the Numbers of Homeless Young People

Difficulties with estimates
Estimating the number of homeless young people is a difficult—if not perilous—task. Surveys provide most of the information available, but there are problems with the methods and data. So-called double and multiple counting allegedly occurs in surveys when young people are counted at a shelter or refuge that has

turned them away, then counted again when seeking accommodation elsewhere. It does not appear that young people who have been turned away are 'tagged' or in any way identifiable when seeking accommodation at another shelter. Double counting is usually mentioned in the context of exaggerating the number of homeless people, but it is difficult to ascertain the extent of any overstatement. Furthermore, there are other factors which act to negate or cancel any alleged inflation of the estimates due to double counting. Such factors include an indeterminate number of young people who do not seek accommodation from agencies, those who are turned away at one agency and who do not or cannot seek accommodation elsewhere, the fact that not all agencies respond to the surveys and that surveys tend to be program specific and thus do not include agencies which are funded from different sources (Fopp 1989b: 355–9). It is likely that the double counting is more than compensated for by the factors which deflate or understate the estimates.

Another disadvantage of surveys of accommodation services arises from the treatment of the data, namely, the extrapolation of information obtained from a survey conducted for a month or two to obtain a yearly estimate. This method is clearly subject to inaccuracies in both directions; the data may over or understate the extent of homelessness among young people. Such difficulties may be overcome by surveying for a year or for at least three or six months, without extrapolation, to obtain an annual figure.

National surveys

There have been several national surveys which provide some indication of the extent of homelessness among young people. The evaluation of the national Youth Services Scheme (YSS) from October 1980 to September 1981 is mentioned here because it was a survey of all young people requesting accommodation from agencies funded under the program. During the twelve months of the survey 12 382 young people sought accommodation. Noteworthy is the fact that YSS was intended for under-18-year-olds although some older young people were accommodated (Sheridan 1983: Appendix 1, 3).

The next major national survey was undertaken by the National Youth Coalition for Housing which conducted a survey of accommodation services funded under the Supported Accommodation Assistance Program (SAAP). This survey, conducted between July 1986 and June 1987, found that in the 103 services (of the 280 which responded) there were 13 709 referrals of which 9245 were able to be accommodated (Gardiner and O'Neil 1987).

As far as I have been able to ascertain, the above are the only national surveys which have been undertaken over a year. Valuable information has been provided by shorter national surveys of accommodation services for young people, and particular those funded by the Supported Accommodation Assistance Program (SAAP). For example, a national survey, which was conducted between April and June 1987, revealed that 3360 young people were accommodated in youth services funded under SAAP. This figure excludes data from the Australian Capital Territory, Queensland and Western Australia and incomplete data from Victoria (Chesterman 1988: 51). It, therefore, understates the number of young people using such services. In addition, 24 per cent of the 10 419 who used services under the General Supported Accommodation Program (a sub-program of SAAP) were under 25 years (Chesterman 1988: 18, 53). Thus, 5833 young people were accommodated in SAAP services in the three months from April to June 1987. This number excludes any data about under-25-year-olds from the Women's Emergency Support Program (another sub-program of SAAP).

A one-night national census (SAAP 1991a: 18), with an 80 per cent response rate, found that out of a total of 6687 people accommodated, 2698 or 28.5 per cent were young people. A two-week national survey of SAAP services between 17 and 30 September 1990 revealed that an average of 10 030 people were accommodated on an average night of whom 2009 or 20 per cent were young people (SAAP 1991b: 6). These data do not represent an accurate estimate of the number of homeless young people in Australia because there may have been additional young people under 25 years who were catered for in other services (for example, in services for single men and single women), and because only four-fifths of agencies responded (SAAP 1991b: 4).

State surveys

There has been at least one annual survey undertaken at the State level. A survey of SAAP services in Victoria between July 1990 and June 1991 (Community Services Victoria 1991: 6) revealed that of the 8041 people accommodated in SAAP funded (but community-managed) services, 3328 were young people (41.4 per cent). An interesting aspect of this Victorian data is that, in addition to the 8041 people accommodated, there were also 3500 accompanying children. The vast majority (80.7 per cent) were under 9 years (Community Services Victoria 1991: 6). The remaining 657 children were over 10 years. This highlights the fact that not all children and young people who are homelesss live independently of their parents; that, in this survey, a small proportion of young people's homelessness is a function of their parents housing crisis or homelessness.

State surveys reveal a much higher number of young people accommodated than do national surveys. Epitomising this variety of data is a six-month survey undertaken by the New South Wales Youth Accommodation Association (Coffey and Wadelton 1991). The data for the years 1987–1990 are presented in table 1 (Coffey and Wadelton 1991: 5).

The table reveals a gradual increase in requests for accommodation in the four years of the survey. In 1990 there were 15 192 requests of which 6076 were met. The 6076 young people accommodated from this six-month New South Wales study is a much higher figure than that derived from the SAAP one-night census and two-week survey. The New South Wales data highlights the need for care when using a one-night census or two-week survey to estimate the extent of homelessness. The large number of unmet requests means that the total number of requests may be an unreliable measure of the number of homeless young people because of possible double counting. It does, however, tell us something of significance. It is an important indicator of the extent of the difficulties young people face and of their acute need for more accommodation (which may not necessarily be in shelters and refuges).

Table 1 Demand for Accommodation in New South Wales, 1987–1990

	1987	1988	1989	1990
Requests:	13145	13993	14840	15192
Requests met:	3159	4272	5384	6076
Requests:				
Metro	9634	10472	11310	11196
Country	3511	3521	3530	3996
Crisis	7575	9133	10690	11292
M/Long	5570	4860	4150	3900
<16		2154	4268	4916
Male			8482	8994
Female			6358	6198
Requests met:				
Metro	1493	2613	3733	4254
Country	1666	1659	1651	1822
Crisis	2517	3592	4666	5256
M/Long	642	680	718	820
<16		1069	1570	2256
Male			3281	3466
Female			2103	2611

Indirect methods of estimating

Another method of estimating the number of young people who are homeless in the broader sense uses Australian Bureau of Statistics (ABS) data on the number of young people who are not members of a family, who are unemployed and who are between the ages of 15 and 24 years. On the assumption that most people in this category would have as their principal source of income a government pension, it was estimated in February 1988 that there were approximately 41 000 unemployed young people aged between 15 and 24 years who were homeless or 'at risk' of becoming homeless (Fopp 1989a: 363). At the same time it was estimated that there were 8500 young people aged 12–15 who were homeless. This data, showing 50 000 young people to be homeless or 'at risk', was used by the National Inquiry into Homeless Children (Human Rights and Equal Opportunity Commission 1989) as the basis of the estimate that there were 20 000–25 000 children and young people under 18 years who were homeless. Using the same method in June 1990, it was estimated that there were 40 000 young people who were homeless or 'at risk' (Fopp 1991: 7; Fopp 1992b: 28).

A more recent attempt to estimate the number of homeless young people has been made by Mackenzie and Chamberlain (1992). This estimate is based on Victorian SAAP data which showed that there were 1092 young people in SAAP accommodation. Mackenzie and Chamberlain (1992: 20) attempted to calculate what proportion of the young homeless population were accommodated in SAAP services. Using evidence from various sources, they concluded that between 20 and 33 per cent of young people were in SAAP accommodation from which they derived a minimum estimate of 12 750, and a maximum estimate of 21 000, preferring 15 000–19 000 per night. This latest attempt is long overdue and is the first of what is hoped will be a 'second generation' of estimates.

A balanced approach

Where does this leave the estimate of the number of homeless young people in Australia? Estimates to date have been based on a diversity of definitions, differing evidence from local and state and national studies, varying time-spans including every permutation of days and months and respondents of different ages. Not surprisingly, important assumptions have had to be made in most of the estimates derived from the research.

The available estimates are from different perspectives and should all contribute to our understanding of the enormous housing problems faced by young people. It is important to recognise what the research actually does highlight while at the same time being fully aware of its limitations. For example, SAAP surveys are limited to SAAP services (thus excluding young people in other services) and omit the literally homeless and, therefore, cannot be used as an indicator of the homeless population overall. SAAP data do not include young people who are 'at risk' or should leave home because of abuse or violence, but cannot. Likewise the 40 000 figure of 12–24-year-olds who are homeless or 'at risk' (June 1990) does not—and cannot—reveal how many are homeless (according to the definition used) and how many are 'at risk'. This does not detract from the usefulness of the estimate, provided the assumptions, definitions and data on which it is based are understood and weighed when using the data.

The official estimate being used by the government is 20 000. In an attachment to a recent press release, the Minister for the Aged, Family and Health Services, Peter Staples (1992a), claimed that:

> *It is estimated that 20,000 young people aged between 12 and 24 years are homeless.*
>
> Of that 20,000 young people, an estimated 4,000 (i.e. 20%) have no shelter at all (i.e. living on the streets, in deserted buildings, railway carriages, under bridges, etc).
>
> The remaining 16,000 homeless young people are believed to be living in private dwellings without security of tenure or moving between various forms of temporary shelter, including friends, relatives, youth refuges, night shelters, boarding houses, hostels and other forms of emergency accommodation.

The source of this estimate, and of the 4000 literally homeless and those homeless although accommodated on any one night, is not cited in the documentation. However, the total number is consistent with Mackenzie Chamberlain's estimate of 19 000 homeless young people aged between 12 and 24 years per night. The National Housing Strategy data must also be considered. They show that in 1988 there were 77 200 young people aged 15–24 years who were renting privately and spending 30 per cent of their income on accommodation (1991: 33).

It seems then that youth homelessness policies must be directed at a very small proportion of young people who are literally homeless, a larger proportion who are sheltered but remain homeless, and a much greater number who are in housing stress and 'at risk'. It must be remembered that all of these young people have had contact with schools during their life experience.

Causes of Homelessness

Of all the issues relating to the housing difficulties young people face, the causes are the most disputed. One newspaper even claimed that, 'There are 1000 reasons people are on the streets' (*Age*, 8 July 1989). For one commentator writing in the *Sun Herald* (26 February 1989), Australian society has met its nemesis. 'The chickens have come home to roost . . . ' 'We have been chopping away at society's foundation for years. We can hardly express surprise when life's tree collapses for many people.' Another alleged that the cause of homelessness is that young people 'choose' such a lifestyle. For example, one newspaper (*Sydney Morning Herald*, 25 February 1989) suggested that:

> Homeless youth cannot be put in a single category; they are not all drug users or hardened street kids. What they have in common is transience. Lacking permanent homes, they sleep out, go to temporary refuges, stay with friends, live in squats and exchange sex for shelter. In the eastern suburbs and Kings Cross, a vast majority have homes to go to; they are often the children of middle-class parents who've had a marriage breakdown. The children choose to live in the streets.

Contributing factors

Another perspective can be gained from the Report of the National Committee for the Evaluation of the Youth Services Scheme (YSS) entitled, *'One Step Forward': Youth Homelessness & Emergency Accommodation Services* (Sheridan 1983). According to YSS, 'Homeless youth exemplify a transition which has been unsuccessful or beset with problems'. The evaluation explores 'two sets of factors' in explaining the housing problems young people experience. The two sets of factors include 'those situational factors that led to the premature abandonment of the family home and which make reconciliation difficult or even impossible and those external factors that deny a viable self-determination' (Sheridan 1983: 15). In the first category is included 'family conflict, household breakdown, emotional difficulties, drug or alcohol problems, pregnancy, sexual or other forms of physical abuse, school related problems and institutionalisation'. In the external-factors category is included low levels of unemployment benefits for under-18 years and 'none at all for under-16-year-olds', the high cost of rents in the private market, 'a gradual withdrawal of public housing from young people', the discrimination against young people by landlords, the lack of affordable alternative accommodation for young people (including hostels), lack of the requisite skills for independent living, and 'general financial constraints normally experienced by youth and the difficulties incumbent on young people merely as a result of their juvenile status'. The authors of the report note that on occasions the two sets of factors converge:

> Some of these factors such as unemployment might be seen as both situational and external influences, on the one hand building friction within the family home until the person is asked, or chooses, to leave and, on the other, denying a sufficient income for living independent of family or other supports. (Sheridan 1983: 15)

The National Inquiry into Homeless Children found that the 'factors contributing to youth homelessness' (Human Rights and Equal Opportunity Commission 1989: 83) were similar to those of the Sheridan Report. For example, in the relevant sections there are chapters on 'Families under stress', 'Family poverty and isolation', Children in the care of state', 'Youth unemployment', 'The situation of Aboriginal young people' and 'The situation of young refugees'. Burdekin found that some witnesses 'cited rejection of family values as the reason many children decide to leave home: the desire to live with a boyfriend, to smoke, not to work, to take drugs or alcohol, not to assist with household chores, and so on' (Human Rights and Equal Opportunity Commission 1989: 86). However, the inquiry found that only a 'small proportion of young people may leave home for these kinds of reasons', and continued: 'The evidence given in every State and Territory, however, established that far more serious and complex reasons are usually involved'. Overall, the National Inquiry into Homeless Children concluded that the factors involved in the causes of youth homelessness were attributable to such matters as the lack of support for families, poverty, and unemployment, the compounded disadvantage of the indigenous population and the special circumstances of refugees. The inquiry also highlighted alleged abdication by states and territories of the responsibility for young people (who should have been) in their care.

Another explanation emphasises the broader structural causes of homelessness such as unemployment, under-employment, low incomes, inadequate and insecure benefits and pensions from the social security system and the dearth of affordable, appropriate, secure accommodation and the difficulty of gaining access to housing in the private and public housing arena. An excellent summary of the broader structural issues is presented by Elizabeth Morgan and Carol Vincent (1987). The authors claim that the 'current housing crisis experienced by youth is not a consequence of particular parents abdicating their responsibilities, of the breakdown of the family or of young people suddenly becoming rebellious'. They continue, 'it is a complex interaction of the following factors':

- the recent creation of 'adolescence' as a period of dependence on families;
- a changing social structure which offers little support to families;
- an economic system which seriously disadvantages many people, and contributes to rising unemployment;
- a society which creates expectations for a standard of living which is unachievable to many young people;
- the reflection of an international economic crisis. (Morgan and Vincent 1987: 22)

Thus, the issue of the causes of homelessness is a contentious but important one. Whatever those who advance the various causes may think, explanations become significant political tools in the debate about homelessness and, more particularly, in the solutions proposed to deal with such problems. Not only is there disagreement about the causes, but the causes have implications for the remedies proposed. Presumably most policy makers will advocate the distribution of the largest amount of resources to the most important cause (Fopp 1992c)—or, at least, their perception of the most important cause. Of concern is the possibility that personal views or a pandering to misinformed popular opinion, rather than the most important substantiated causes, will motivate the way in which money is spent. This may exacerbate rather than alleviate the problem.

Misconceptions

A popular misconception is that young people choose to leave home. The evidence of the National Inquiry into Homeless Children revealed that the great majority of young people do not choose to leave home. Two quotations from witnesses to the inquiry suffice to support this view. The first is from a representative of an agency working with young people: 'Some people often say that kids leave home. But in most cases, home leaves them' (Human Rights and Equal Opportunity Commission 1989: 85). The second is taken from the report of a consultant to the inquiry who interviewed 100 homeless young people: 'It is clear from the young people's accounts that leaving home was not a result of a whim; rather, their stories are reflective of ongoing and deep-seated difficulties' (Human Rights and Equal Opportunity Commission 1989: 87). The evidence indicates that the claim that young people choose to leave home—whatever that might mean—is inaccurate, misleading and unfair to the vast majority of young people.

Accompanying the view that young people choose to leave home is the view that young people are less committed to so-called family values. The evidence suggests that young people have positive attitudes to notions of family and long-standing relationships (Amato 1985; Edgar 1985; Hartley 1991) despite any disruption and trauma associated with parental separation and divorce (Hartley 1991; Macdonald 1991).

There is another misconception about youth homelessness, namely, that young people are leaving home in droves, or that young people are leaving home at earlier ages than in the past in order to establish themselves independently prior to marriage (Walters 1982: 3). Demographic analysis of surveys conducted in 1971 and 1982 provides only limited support for this view. Comparisons of surveys in this period 'provide a conservative estimate of the decrease in leaving home ... of 0.2 years among sons and a possible increase of 0.5 years among daughters' (Young 1987: 33). This means that, compared with 1971, sons were leaving home a little earlier and daughters were staying up to six months longer. Evidence collected between 1981 and 1986 suggests that young people were remaining at their parents' home for longer periods in the early to mid 1980s

(Kilmartin 1987: 40). It is apparent that this same trend continued in the late 1980s (Hartley 1990: 67–9). Data suggest that 10 per cent of 15–19 year olds, and almost 50 per cent of those aged 20–24 years, live independently of their parents (Attridge 1992: 5). Thus, the statement that young people are leaving home at an earlier age in order to become independent is inconsistent with the evidence available.

Frequently, the method adopted is to assess the attributes of the young people who are homeless and then extrapolate the cause(s). Thus, if young people are drug-users, have broken the law, are parents, are unemployed, have seemingly irreconcilable differences with their parents or spouses/partners, then these attributes are regarded as the causes of their homelessness.

There are two flaws with this argument. Firstly, personal attributes do not necessarily constitute causes. Many people have living skills which leave a lot to be desired but such people do not necessarily become homeless. Likewise, most parents will inform inquirers that at one or another time their children have been wilful but not all of these 'wilful' children become homeless. Furthermore, to confuse or conflate personal attributes with the causes of homelessness does not address the direction of the causes (that is, whether a causes b or vice versa).

Is it possible to adjudicate between the competing claims about the many causes of homelessness? Does the main cause of homelessness reside in the alleged characteristics (usually regarded as inadequacies) of individuals or in the broader structures of our society, in under- and unemployment, and the lack of affordable, appropriate, safe and secure housing? The first cause is known as the residual explanation (that the location of homelessness resides in the individual); the second is known as the structural explanation (Dwyer 1989: 12; Fopp 1992b: 26–30). Categorising the respective causes in the above manner assists in managing the evidence, but what is also needed is a method to determine which of the two has the greater explanatory power.

There are several paths down which we might proceed at this juncture. A first step might be to recall that estimates show that three-quarters of young people who were homeless or at risk of becoming homeless are over 16 years. Three surveys, for example, indicate that relatively small percentages of under-16-

year-olds are homeless (Coffey and Wadelton 1991: 5; Community Services Victoria 1991: 20; SAAP 1991: 20). Thus, homelessness or being at risk appears to increase with age so that most people who face acute housing problems are likely to be over 16 years. Such an assessment does not diminish the needs of those under 16 years but does help to identify the age group with the largest numbers of homeless young people.

The next step is to recognise that most young people leave home and do not become homeless and are not even at risk (Fopp 1992b: 28–9). For most young people, leaving home does not cause homelessness or a housing crisis. This is an important point because it challenges one of the central assumptions in the debate about 'youth homelessness'—that leaving home causes homelessness—which seemingly endorses the merging of personal attributes or behaviour on the one hand, and broader causes of homelessness on the other. If leaving home does not cause homelessness for most young people over 16 years, why is it regarded as a cause for those who are homeless? This observation prompts another question: what is the experience of young people who leave home but are not homeless or at risk which is denied their homeless counterparts?

What distinguishes those young people over 16 years who leave home and do become homeless is their exclusion from the labour market. This prevents them from securing an income which is stable and sufficient to meet living expenses including rent. Attridge (1992: 6) summarises the importance of lack of income in this way: 'Inadequate income is the greatest barrier faced by young people in securing housing independence'. Because over 65 per cent of young people rent in the public sector and very high proportions pay over 35 per cent of their income in rent, Attridge concluded that 'the priority for assistance is obviously young people in the private sector. They comprise 75.1 per cent of all young people paying more than 35 per cent and 72.3 per cent of those paying more than 50 per cent' of their income in rent. The report also noted that young people 'in other rental housing also need urgent assistance with 12.8 per cent facing housing costs in excess of 50 per cent of their income' (Attridge 1992: 11).

In Australia, income is largely a function of the demand and supply of labour. Income is inextricably related to employment and unemployment, under-employment and low youth wages. The loss of 300 000 jobs previously undertaken by young people in the past twenty-five years (Robinson 1992: 6), the dramatic increase in part-time employment, the decrease in full-time employment, unemployment for increasingly long periods and inadequate income support while unemployed, explain the inadequate and low incomes which exclude young people from the housing market or preclude them from participating successfully (Dwyer 1989: 12).

While unemployment and under-employment are the primary factors resulting in homelessness among over-16-year-olds, homelessness can itself adversely affect labour-market participation. Thus, 'Homelessness and unemployment are inextricably linked. Young people have been unable to get work or access to training because they do not have adequate and secure housing' (Staples 1992a). Furthermore, unemployment and under-employment inter-link with the housing market so that inequities in the labour market and the housing market are compounded.

The structural explanation for homelessness has the additional merit of explaining the compounded disadvantage of some sub-groups within the homeless and at-risk population. For example, the aggravated disadvantage of young women (Gardiner and O'Neil 1987; Ford 1988; Barclay et al. 1991; Econsult 1992a), young mothers (Macdonald 1991), young people of Aboriginal descent (Synott 1987), young people from non-English-speaking backgrounds (Meekosha and Jakubowicz 1987) and young people with disabilities, and young people from rural areas (Breen 1987; Quixley 1990), is explained more effectively in terms of the broader, structural inequalities experienced by such young people, including inequities in the labour and housing market, socially constructed notions of family, race and ethnicity and the expectations associated with them.

The conclusion reached in this discussion is that broad structural features best explain the causes of homelessness of young people over 16 years. For young people under 16 years leaving home is likely to cause homelessness because they would not normally be expected to have the resources to become independent and self-sufficient. Because a significant number of young people in this age group leave their parents' residence precisely because they are victims of violence (broadly understood and including what are now regarded as sexual crimes) leaving home cannot be regarded as typifying the residual explanation. In fact, many would regard domestic violence and crimes (including sexual crimes), against the person as structural in origin, as endemic to the prevalent notion of the family. Thus, what might seem a residual cause can be a structural one.

There are two final points which require emphasis. First it is important to identify the main or primary causes of homelessness to ensure that symptoms are not confused with causes and to ensure that any available funding addresses the main cause or causes. The second point is a qualification, namely, that while the broader, economic and social issues have been identified as possessing the greatest explanatory power, this does not mean that individual traits and means of mediating circumstances are not implicated at all in the explanation of homelessness offered here. Of course personal attributes play a part. The point is that they are alleged to play a much larger part in explaining homelessness than is justified.

Possible Solutions

Certainly until 1985, the main strategy adopted to address the housing problems faced by young people has been to provide refuges or shelters operated by non-profit, community housing organisations. These organisations offer various forms of accommodation ranging from crisis to long-term supported accommodation. Emergency or crisis accommodation in refuges or shelters may be available for several days while longer-term accommodation may be available for up to twelve months' duration. The shelters and refuges were initiatives of the community sector which, in the mid to late 1970s, recognised that shelters for homeless men were catering for an increasing number of young people (Jordan 1978; Hart 1979; Fopp 1981). This influx of young people in accommodation previously targeting older homeless men coincided with increasing unemployment among young people and high inflation with diminishing economic growth (Cummins and Wilson 1977; Cairns Committee for Homeless Persons 1979; Council of Social Service of Tasmania 1979; Chappel 1980; Duffield et al. 1979;

Wagstaff 1980; Victorian Consultative Committee on Social Development 1979; Walters 1982).

Prior to 1985, funding for the community organisations was provided by the federal and state governments in a myriad of programs from a multitude of departments. The resulting confusion and frustration of the community organisations led to the development of a program which streamlined the previous programs into the Supported Accommodation Assistance Program (SAAP). SAAP operated under three sub-programs: the General Supported Accommodation Program (known as GSAP) which targeted families and single men and women), the Youth Supported Accommodation Program (YSAP) and the Women's Emergency Support Porgram (WESP). Established in 1985, SAAP was jointly funded by the Commonwealth, and states and territories, and had the following aim: ' . . . to assist men, women, young people and their dependants who are either permanently homeless or temporarily homeless as a result of crisis and who need such support to move towards independent living where possible and appropriate (Howe 1985).

After an extensive national evaluation (Chesterman 1988) the first version of SAAP (known as SAAP Mark I) was modified. The next version (known as SAAP Mark II) was introduced in 1989. Its aims are outlined below:

> The primary principle of the program is to ensure that the homeless people in crisis in Australia have access to adequate and appropriate transitional supported accommodation and related support services. In implementing this principle, assistance will also reflect the following detailed principles:
> (i) the focus of the program will be on transitional assistance. Services will be designed to be of varying duration and levels of support to meet the needs of individuals to move towards independent living or other appropriate alternatives;
> (ii) the emphasis will be on ensuring individuals retain maximum independence;
> (iii) there will be an early assessment of client's needs, referral to more appropriate services or programs where required and available;

(iv) services will be available to all sections of the community irrespective of sex, marital status, race, religion, disability or life situation;
(v) services will be sensitive to the problems of homelessness, domestic violence and personal crisis and will actively work to enhance the dignity, self-esteem and independence of clients;
(vi) services will assist clients in ways which recognise the individual needs of clients, develop clients' independence and enhance their own support network; and
(vii) priority will be given to services involved in direct service provision for homeless people in crisis and whose focus is on assistance for individual clients.

As a response to the National Inquiry into Homeless Children (Human Rights and Equal Opportunity Commission 1989) funding for services to young people was increased (Department of Health, Housing and Community Services 1992). The actual expenditure is shown in table 2 (Staples 1992b).

Table 2 Services for Homeless Youth, 1991–92

State	Number of Services SAAP	YSJS	SAAP a and b $million	Youth Social Justice Strategy (YSJS) a $million	Total Funding a $million
NSW	188	37	20.7	3.2	23.9
Vic.	147	42	11.1	2.4	13.5
QLD	74	20	8.3	1.6	9.9
SA	52	9	5.5	1.8	7.3
WA	37	8	4.1	0.8	4.9
Tas.	15	0	2.0	NIL	2.0
ACT	15	5	1.9	0.4	2.2
NT	4	1	0.5	0.4	0.8
Total	532	122	$54.1 million	$10.4 million	$64.5 million

a These figures represent combined Commonwealth/State contributions.
b Supported Accommodation Assistance Program

Supported accommodation (usually via SAAP) has become the main means of providing housing for young people. This program has involved more than the provision of crisis or emergency accommodation in refuges and shelters. Increasingly agencies are developing programs which are medium to long term (6–12 months). In this later development support tends to be provided by outreach or detached workers who encourage and advocate for young people in their increasingly independent accommodation (McDivett 1986; Barrett 1987).

There are thus three forms of supported accommodation.

- Short-term supported accommodation in refuges or shelters with varying levels of adult supervision;
- Medium (3–6 months) and long-term (up to 12 months) accommodation with support provided by outreach workers operating from an external base;
- Support and other non-accommodation services to young people in independent, long-term accommodation (for example, public housing or private rental) by outreach workers operating from an external base.

Most of the youth housing remains in the short-term, adult supervised, supported accommodation area, with the long-term accommodation and outreach models only gradually increasing. This emphasis is the result of previous funding priorities and continues despite the fact that Burdekin stressed the need for long-term accommodation, that the number of services providing medium- to long-term accommodation has increased (Department of Health, Housing and Community Services: 1992), and that one of the major issues in the recent and national SAAP Review was the lack of exit points from SAAP accommodation services (Econsult 1992). Because of the paucity of long-term affordable, appropriate and safe shelters, young people in medium accommodation are unable to move out, remain in all levels of SAAP services and cause other young people to be turned away.

Some young people require various forms of support when living independently. This is most practically and efficiently provided by outreach workers who advocate for young people to ensure that they receive their income entitlements and who attempt, after consultation, to link young people to mainstream education and training, employment and health and housing services. It is generally recognised that such services are not 'user-friendly' to young people who are homeless or who are experiencing housing crisis. For this reason specialist services have been established.

One particular problem faced by young people who are homeless or in housing crisis is that it is difficult, if not impossible, for them to continue their education or to benefit from training programs. In one program in South Australia a school recognised this need, conducted a survey of the young people and their housing needs, sought the assistance of the South Australian Housing Trust to provide houses, and worked with a local housing organisation to provide the necessary support for their students. While it is true that young people required various supports (including child-care), their basic and prior need was for affordable and stable accommodation. The students' view was that affordable and safe accommodation was an essential pre-condition of their attempt to remain at school (Fopp et al. 1990: 25–6).

One conclusion that can be reached concerning the solutions is that they seem to be based more on residualist than structural explanations. For example, the emphasis on supported accommodation and the lack of exit points both within and outside SAAP services seems to point more to managing the victims of homelessness rather than addressing the structural issues which cause the problem. Moreover, the discrimination against young people in the private sector remains (National Housing Strategy 1992: 29). State housing authorities have not allocated facilities to young people on a proportionate basis. (Cunnew and Downie 1986; Fopp et al. 1990; Attridge 1992; Fopp 1992a).

The combined effect of the emphasis in SAAP of supported accommodation, the paucity of exit points, the emphasis on addressing the needs of under-18-year-olds, and particularly under-16-year-olds, and the failure to address issues of discrimination in private sector housing and access to public sector housing, not only suggests that the residualist explanation dominates policy decisions (even if by default), but that policy formulation has been fragmented and has sometimes compounded the problems for young people. It has also involved inappropriate adult intrusion into the personal affairs of young people in ways which limit their independence (Young Women's Housing Collective 1991: 24–5; Neil and Fopp 1992: 167). It has helped to underline the deviance attributed to such young people. Such a conclusion is not a justification for less funding but for more; it is an argument for policies which dramatically increase the access of young people to long-term, independent, affordable and safe and secure housing, a secure income and all the resources to improve their circumstances including assistance to allow them to gain access to education and training programs, and employment. Any lesser solution will compound the problem rather than cure it and ignores the accommodation preferences stated in every survey—few though they be—which has asked young people about their housing needs and preferences (Youth Affairs Council 1983: 61–4; National Youth Coalition for Housing 1987: 5; Fopp 1987: 17; Housing Tasmania 1998: 4–11; deVries and Tunnell 1990; South Australian Youth Housing Network 1992: 32; Fopp 1992c)

Education and Training

There is another urgent question: assuming that young people have acquired accommodation or are settled in their interim accommodation, is it possible to overcome their severe disadvantage in the labour market? This is an important question for several reasons, first, because disadvantage in the labour market most adequately explains homelessness or housing crisis, and second, because of long-term and appropriate housing as an important pre-condition for being able to compete in the labour market or for places in the education and training system.

There can be little doubt that some young people without homes are students—or want to be. For example, in a 1983 study Sheridan et al. (Appendix 19–20) found that 18 per cent or 991 (of 5539) young people in accommodation services were students, of whom nearly 70 per cent were attending school. In a census of SAAP (1990: 22) services in 1989, approximately 14 per cent of young people in accommodation services indicated that they were receiving Independent AUSTUDY with the Young Homeless Allowance. Thus, it is reasonable to assume that 14 per cent of the young people were students. A smaller

Western Australian survey (de Vries and Tunnel 1990: 36) found that a quarter of their sample were attending school or about to attend school. The Elizabeth re-entry program in South Australia revealed that all the young people in receipt of Independent AUSTUDY under the provision for homeless young people were either 'fairly keen' or 'very keen' to pursue their studies, with the latter double that of the former (Fopp et al. 1990: 26). While the numbers surveyed were small (33), three-quarters indicated that they returned to school to further their education and to obtain a job or that furthering their career prospects was the main reason for returning to school (Fopp et al. 1990: 24). However, just under a third said they would 'possibly' or 'probably' have to leave school if they experienced housing problems and half indicated that housing was the major need if they were to continue their education (Fopp et al. 1990: 22).

Clearly, if young people who have been homeless or have experienced housing crisis are to compete in the shrinking youth labour market it is imperative that they acquire skills and experience which will increase their chances of success. The young people interviewed at Elizabeth West certainly explained their return to school in such terms. Thus, once secure accommodation has been attained, it is imperative that young people are granted the opportunity to study. Long-term, affordable, safe and secure housing is a pre-condition but there are other essential prerequisites once this basic need has been met. Such requirements include a sense of security and well-being, a place conducive to study, an adequate income, transport, and, where necessary, child care which includes provision for sick children.

Training is an integral aspect of the remedy for homelessness. As used here, 'training' refers to the specific (usually short-term) programs which are designed to improve skills and competencies in order to enhance a person's competitiveness in the labour market. SkillShare exemplifies training as intended here and is particularly relevant because it is targeted at those who have been unemployed for long periods and at the most disadvantaged groups. There is some evidence to suggest that training from SkillShare increases the chances of becoming employed by up to 50 per cent although these results are more relevant to the first four months after completion of the course than thereafter (SkillShare and Department of Education and Training 1992: 2).

In July 1992 the Federal Government announced a training initiative for young people who were homeless or 'at risk'. Known as the Job Placement and Employment Program (JPET), this training program was set up because homeless young people have difficulty in gaining access to existing programs. JPET was also a response to the difficulties they encounter in finding employment. 'Until now finding employment and training opportunities for disadvantaged young people has been difficult to approach in any systematic way' (Staples 1992a). It is intended that JPET should be operated by community groups (usually local youth housing organisations) with experience in working with young people who are homeless or at risk.

Education and training cannot be the only antidotes to unemployment and, therefore, homelessness. Education has always been a key structural mechanism for social placement in Australia, for the sorting out or filtering of students into the workforce according to their abilities in the hierarchy of knowledge. Likewise, training can be seen to be a further refinement of this process by tailoring the pool of labour to the demands of those who supply employment in a more sophisticated manner. Even if the chances of acquiring a job by undertaking a SkillShare program are increased by 50 per cent (SkillShare and Department of Employment, Education and Training 1992: 2) such training will not automatically assist a large proportion of participants to gain employment since the entire reservoir of unemployed cannot all get jobs no matter how finely tuned their skills are to the job market. They may be forced to enter the training merry-go-round as they enhance and refine skills for which there are many more applicants than jobs.

Thus inequalities in the labour market compound the inequalities in the housing market. The salient point is that homeless young people are even more disadvantaged than most; if they are to compete successfully it is essential that, at least, they build on previous and acquired new skills. In the JPET program they also have contact with workers who can advocate on their behalf.

Conclusion

This chapter has explored the most popular explanations for homelessness among young people and has highlighted their inadequacies. Most importantly, it has explored the connection between the dominant explanations of housing problems, on the one hand, and the solutions which have been implemented to alleviate and remedy the hardship many young people experience, on the other. Until very recently the solutions have been based on residual explanations. The contention here is that homelessness among young people will not be resolved while it is seen as a problem caused by young people. It will only be resolved when the structural causes are addressed, when it is realised that young people have housing problems because of the broader structural malaise. It is sometimes said that young people run away from home; some say that home has run away from them. Have the broader social structures run away from young people too? A careful analysis of homelessness certainly raises this question. The legitimate and now well identified needs of young people beg an answer and above all action. One area where action is urgently needed is the education system.

7

The Social Costs of Youth Homelessness

The discussion of social costs in this chapter will focus on those impacts of youth homelessness, for both individuals and communities, which generally cannot be measured in monetary terms, or if they can, are better considered in a social rather than an economic framework.

At first glance, 'social cost' and 'cost to society' are reasonably straightforward notions and most people intuitively know what they mean. However, on closer reflection, they are quite complex, and approaches to such costs may vary, not least because they are closely related to personal and social values, and to how we define the well-being of society.

Setting a Framework

The simple framework adopted for this discussion is that costs in general may be monetary or non-monetary, and they are borne by both individuals and communities. In our society, 'cost' is usually associated with money and there is in fact a very complex and comprehensive economic theory of costs. However, it is widely recognised that there are costs which cannot be measured in narrow monetary terms or in somewhat broader economic terms. For example, while monetary costs of youth homelessness include the amount expended on benefits and allowances for those who qualify as homeless, we cannot put a monetary cost on the reduction in quality of life for young people while they are homeless. Yet this is a fundamental consideration. Many social costs are of this nature, and even if by some means they could be measured in monetary terms, it is clear that we need to think about such costs in the broad context of social and moral values, rather than within an economic framework, because they involve questions of social justice and equity.

Costs may be direct or indirect. For example, poverty, the inevitable partner of homelessness, may lead to an increase in crime and a decrease in general health levels across the community; a much less direct and less tangible cost is loss of faith and growing cynicism and uncertainty among young people.

Both individuals and communities have to bear costs and economists usually refer to these as private and public costs. For example, the educational opportunities and life chances of young people who are homeless are generally severely restricted. The cost that they bear is to miss out on both the intrinsic and external rewards of education. However, the community also bears a cost when the potential skills and contribution of individual people are lost. This example also illustrates that social costs often come from lost opportunities or unfulfilled potential.

A chain of costs: unemployment, poverty and homelessness

Homelessness is so closely associated with poverty, and very frequently with unemployment, that it is difficult to separate out social costs which result from being without a home, and those which derive from having very little money. In many cases, it is not relevant to attempt such a distinction. If young people are homeless, they are (with possibly a very few exceptions) living in poverty, and the great majority are either unemployed or they are students. The close connection between young people being unemployed and being homeless has been well documented (Hirst 1989; Boyce 1992), and there are major debilitating effects of poverty and unemployment which can be seen as social costs.

Not surprisingly because of their close association, youth homelessness itself is often seen as a social cost of unemployment, or of general economic stress on families and the failure of society to provide affordable accommodation options for young people living independently of their families. What we identify as a social cost depends to some extent on the point of focus in an interrelated chain.

Nevertheless, the social costs of homelessness are not necessarily synonymous with those of poverty and unemployment. Living on the streets, or in very inadequate accommodation, or constantly having to shift, is a different experience from being poor but having a stable place to live. The additional impact of instability and lack of support is profound, particularly for young people.

The treatment of homelessness

Elsewhere in this book, it is argued that the way homelessness is defined in its turn defines the way in which it is analysed and responded to. In a summary of the various definitions of and points of view about youth homelessness, Chamberlain and Mackenzie (1992) make a point which is particularly relevant for the present discussion of social costs. They point out that the range of definitions of homelessness in the literature, from very inclusive to much less inclusive, is frequently explained by the fact that different groups and individuals formulate operational definitions for a range of practical purposes. The practical purpose in this chapter is to discuss social costs and therefore a tight definition of homelessness does not seem appropriate. Rather, the focus is on three key aspects of youth homelessness—absence of stable accommodation, poverty and lack of support.

For younger children, lack of support is a crucial element. This includes lack of support from the state as guardian. A significant proportion of young homeless people have been wards of the state (Hirst 1989) and 'involvement with corrective or protective custodial programs' seems to predispose young people to becoming homeless (Victorian Family and Children's Services Council 1991). Lack of preparation and provision in 'exit planning' often ensures that they have no secure accommodation to go to, very little backup from friends or adults they can rely on, a minimum of income support and few resources to plan for the future. They exit into homelessness (Taylor 1990).

In thinking about social costs, it is important to consider the broad implications and meaning of homelessness. It is significant that we talk about 'homelessness' rather than 'houselessness' or lack of shelter. Being homeless means the absence of the total 'package' which is implied in our concept of 'home'. Neil (1992) summarises the attributes of a home which have been identified in the literature. They include security of tenure linked to a sense of belonging and stability; security for each member of the household against external and internal threats; decent standards which vary from culture to culture but which as a minimum should not undermine health or contribute to any other disadvantages; and a degree of affordability such that paying for accommodation doesn't mean that other necessities of life cannot be afforded. Other attributes of a home are an environment where people can establish their own relationships with others they like, opportunities for freely chosen privacy, some degree of control and autonomy, accessibility to services, and appropriateness to the age and particular needs of inhabitants.

Homes thus provide not only for physical needs but also for social and personal needs, and an analysis of social costs needs to take account of what the absence of a home means in these terms. One group of homeless young people described homes as places where they are understood and respected, have some freedom to make their own decisions about social relationships and personal habits, where people care about them, where there is openness and honesty, they are able to exercise responsibility, and basic physical needs are met (Beed 1991).

Media response following the Human Rights and Equal Opportunity Commission Report (1989) on homeless children has helped to raise public awareness about youth homelessness. However, it also tended to encourage a stereotype of 'street kids' and to establish 'homelessness' as a catch-all term for young people in a variety of different circumstances. Stereotypes obscure the fact that while there may be common experiences, young people who are homeless are first and foremost, individuals. They vary at the very least according to temperament, motivation, attributes, individual experiences and ability to cope. Some are struggling to stay at school; others have returned to school after years away; the majority have given up on education for a whole range of reasons, including the failure of schools to offer adequate support. Some live on the streets or in squats, some in refuges, some with a series of friends or acquaintances; some have a tenuous hold on private rental accommodation, some live in boarding houses, some move between all of these options.

The experience and the costs of homelessness for young women and young men are often very different. Gender inequalities and the power relationships between females and males in the broader society are frequently starkly evident in the experience of homelessness. Young women are more vulnerable than young men in many ways. They are more likely to have left home because of sexual abuse and more likely to have been raped or sexually abused after they left home (Alder and Sandor 1989); more likely to have the care of children; more likely to be engaged in prostitution; more likely to be in dangerous and abusive relationships in order to survive; more likely to be suffering from sexually transmitted diseases. On the other hand, young males are more likely than young females to be assaulted by the police and to be engaged in physical violence as victims or perpetrators (Alder and Sandor 1989).

Howard (1992: 14) concludes, along with others, that the overall picture for young women is particularly distressing, and that 'their levels of physical and sexual abuse, drug use, signs of emotional distress, suicide attempts, conflicts with both parents and the experience of more violent and less happy homes are all higher than for the males'.

Age is another important variable making for difference in experience and social cost. The age range covered by the terms 'youth' and 'young people' tends to vary. If we take government policies for young people as a guide, they variously include 15–24-year-olds, under-21-year-olds, 12–24-year-olds, and 16–25-year-olds (Cahill and Ewen 1992). For the purpose of this chapter 12–24-year-olds are included, with the focus on 15–24-year-olds, acknowledging that children younger than this are forced to leave home, or in effect have no home. The key point is that age affects the way in which young people cope with homelessness, their general level of maturity, the decisions they make and are able to make, their vulnerability to exploitation, and to some extent the resources they are able to call on. Therefore some personal costs of homelessness for a 13-year-old are different from those of a 22-year-old; community costs will vary also.

Stereotypes about young people who are homeless avoid an understanding of what it means on a day-to-day basis. Some of the implications of the instability, stress and despair which is part of many young people's experience will be discussed in relation to social cost; earlier chapters present individual experiences in greater detail.

Social costs of youth homelessness are discussed in two main sections; the first outlining direct personal costs to young people, the second focusing on the implications for communities, immediate and longer term. A focus on the social costs of homelessness inevitably paints a very negative picture, emphasising such aspects as lack of opportunities, poor health, and the risk of psychological disturbance for young people. However, while there is no positive side to homelessness as such, it must be stressed that there are very many positives about young people who are homeless. They are not totally defined by their homelessness, despite the fact that lack of stable accommodation may dominate their day-to-day life. They have an enormous range of personal attributes, individual skills, competencies, and potential. This book shows that many are determined, resilient, adaptable, creative and inventive.

Costs to Individuals

The personal costs of homelessness for young people are numerous. Instability, poverty and lack of support have devastating effects at any stage of life, but they have particular consequences for 15–24-year-olds, disrupting and distorting expected patterns of development, and restricting options for the future. Some years ago, Keniston (1977) aptly referred to a 'foreclosure of the future' for children living in poverty. Without positive interventions and appropriate support, this too is the private and public cost of youth homelessness—the loss of a future for some young people.

Although costs of homelessness are described under separate headings such as unemployment, and physical and psychological health, they are interrelated and often cumulative. Poor living conditions increase health risks; lack of money increases the possibility that minor illnesses will not be treated and may develop into major illnesses. Hopelessless, alienation, drug use and poor health combine to dramatically increase the risk of suicide.

A crucial life stage

The period between ages 15 and 24 years is a crucial developmental life phase. Young people are expected to accomplish, or at least be on the path towards achieving, some major life tasks. Psychological development, social transitions and changes in status during this period are closely related. It is a time for establishing a sense of personal identity and becoming progressively more independent from parents. Traditionally, there is an expectation that young people will complete schooling and move into the workforce, either directly or after further education or training. The majority leave home during these years to establish households of their own, with or without others. Most form intimate relationships with non-family members. And they assume what Anna Yeatman calls political and civil citizenship (South Australian Youth Incomes Task Force 1988).

Ideally, young people's senses of independence and responsibility develop gradually, with more or less physical and emotional support from parents or other adults who both care for, and about them. Adolescence is a time for testing out views, options and possibilities, preferably in a safe environment. Noller and Patton (1990) describe the ideal family environment for adolescents as one where communication is positive and effective, where adolescents receive strong support from parents, feel free to express their feelings and opinions appropriately, discuss issues, raise conflicts, negotiate about plans and make decisions with a growing sense of their own competence.

Perhaps the most important psychological task begun in adolescence is forming an identity, an answer to the question of 'who am I?' Noller and Callan (1991) suggest that a healthy identity is based on personal exploration of alternative values, attitudes and opinions, and awareness of how one is different from other people. The values of parents, family members, peers, the immediate cultural group and the wider society, are significant influences.

Young people who are homeless often have only experiences of rejection and failure on which to base their sense of identity. The long-term and insidious effects of sexual assault, both before and after leaving home, on personal identity for young women (and less frequently for young men) is profound. A significant proportion of young people who are homeless have little sense of their own value because they have not been valued by people close to them or by a society which, by default or sometimes through deliberate state action, contributes to their homelessness. Again in relation to poverty (but relevant also to homelessness), Keniston says that without the vision of a good life, founded on children's perception of the actual lives and achievements of the adults they know best, they are likely to expect failure of themselves (Keniston 1977). Having said this, we need to acknowledge that many young people have the potential to develop much more positive self-images if they are given understanding and support.

Forming close, intimate and sexual relationships with people outside the family is an important part of growing up. There is much to learn as young people become active sexually and test out relationships, sexual or not. In the best of circumstances, adolescence is often not an easy time as young people face concerns about their own acceptability, and try to negotiate the complex interactions between their own needs and values, expectations of parents, peer pressure, and media images of gender, love and sex.

For young homeless people, there are additional problems. Past experiences may make it difficult for them to trust others, or to care about themselves enough to care for others. In order to survive they are often led into exploitative and dangerous relationships. Young women are particularly vulnerable to sexual and personal exploitation on the street, in refuges, and sometimes from professionals from whom they expect some help (Robson 1992). From a practical point of view, the instability of homelessness and the constant concern with survival puts a lot of pressure on relationships.

It is widely believed that the tasks described above are 'developmental milestones' through which adolescents must pass in order to achieve adulthood and healthy psychological functioning (Noller and Callan, 1991). When they cannot be accomplished, there is a sense of personal and social disorder. High levels of youth unemployment, longer periods spent in education and greater economic stress on families have in recent years changed this period for a growing percentage of young people. The nexus between school and work has been broken, particularly for those who in the past would have left school at the age of 15 or 16, but also increasingly for those who are leaving school at 17 and 18 years. Without employment, the period of dependence on parents, or on the state through Job Search Allowance and Newstart (unemployment benefits), is prolonged. For young homeless people, the pattern of developmental tasks described has little relevance. Some are forced into very early independence without the resources to support themselves; they have neither work, nor parental support and struggle to survive on below-poverty-level allowances.

While the growth of autonomy and independence is an integral part of adolescence, so too is the development of interdependence and responsibility for others. They are core values in a humane and caring society. If young people grow up not being valued and not treated with respect and understanding, we can hardly be surprised if they fail to value interdependence and responsibility for others, or surprised if they regard others as uncaring. It is in fact a tribute to their faith, resilience and optimism that so many of them do not seem to have lost these values.

Unemployment

The link between unemployment and homelessness is well established. Common sense tells us that without employment, it is difficult to afford decent and stable accommodation, and without stable housing, holding down a job is extremely difficult (given that jobs are available, which they are not at present). Consistent and regular participation in a labour market or training program is equally difficult without stable housing. Unemployment, particularly for long periods, has a profound effect on individual and social outcomes. In our society, waged work provides an income for survival, but it also has psychological benefits, including a recognised role in society and a sense of personal and social identity. Some jobs are repetitive, boring, difficult, tedious, or of questionable social use. Nevertheless, at present, waged work remains of central importance in people's lives, and most employment offers, in varying degrees, some benefits beyond a wage. Not least of these benefits are social interaction with people of different age groups and the experience of being treated as a responsible and capable person, both of which contribute to young people's self-esteem.

Access to work is part of becoming independent. It allows a greater range of choices and decisions about one's life. On the other hand, unemployment and lack of an adequate income generally mean being dependent on others, on family, relatives, friends, a partner or the state, so the growing sense of autonomy, independence and responsibility for self which is the right of every young person is less able to develop. Instead there is frequently despair, alienation and lack of confidence.

Unemployment brings disorder in time and place (Allatt and Yeandle 1992). There is a personal and social sense of a 'proper' time for each stage of the family or domestic career, including marriage or living together, underpinned by an expectation that it will coincide with an appropriate stage in the employment career. Unemployment upsets these temporal patterns in life and can ultimately deny people the option of 'settling down', thus 'potentially marginalis(ing) individuals from the progression of their generation through historical time' (Allatt and Yeandle 1992: 107).

At the broadest level, employment allows young people opportunities to participate in the mainstream of life; unemployment excludes them and limits their opportunities. Not only is it difficult to provide for the basic necessities of food, clothing and shelter, but also for the leisure and recreational activities and general cultural experiences which define what being a 'young person' is about. Unemployment and poverty impoverish people (Sinfield 1981).

Restricted educational opportunities

Maas and Hartley (1988) and more recently, Morris and Blaskett (1992) describe the difficulties which young people have in staying at school or returning to study without a stable place to live, and receiving only an AUSTUDY allowance. Later chapters describe these circumstances in detail. If young people have no parental support and limited money, support from the school or the community is essential. Otherwise it is just too difficult to study. In addition to the stress of surviving on a below-poverty-line income, there are also demands of time and money in living independently, including organising accommodation (often moving from one inadequate place to another), planning food, buying, cooking, washing, and juggling payment of bills, all of which may be quite new to young people. On top of all this are pressures and demands of study. School work suffers when time has to be taken out to change accommodation, find part-time work or deal with AUSTUDY problems (Morris and Blaskett 1992).

Many parents are aware of the extra emotional and general support they need to provide for their sons and daughters in the later years of secondary school. Without this support, and a stable place to live, let alone facilities for study, young homeless people are often forced to abandon their education. In the absence of parental support, schools and communities can contribute to young people's sense of security by providing an environment where they are offered care, concern, understanding and practical support (Morris and Blaskett 1992).

In the current economic recession, completing secondary school doesn't necessarily ensure a job or entry into a tertiary institution. However, it is certainly an advantage. In general, as qualifications rise, lower levels of education make it less likely that young people find employment. There are also indications that low education level is one of a number of factors which predict whether young people will have long periods of unemployment (Chapman and Smith 1992). In addition, young people miss out on the intrinsic satisfaction of completing schooling and the possibility of using that education as the foundation for developments of other interests, or for self-employment.

Lack of choices

The exercise of choice is part of growing up. Choices concerning education, employment and future life directions are especially important in adolescence. But as young people move from being under the authority of their parents or guardians to having control over their own lives, so too are choices about when to leave home, where to live, lifestyle and relationships. With an adequate income and/or parental support, young people are able to test out options. They quite frequently first leave home to experiment with living independently, to see what it's like, to give it a go, to see if they can manage (Hartley 1992). Not surprisingly, some return if the going gets too tough, only to leave again later.

Young people who are homeless don't have these options or a choice about when to leave, and many have no sense of control over their lives in general. On the contrary, they lack direction and are constantly at the whim of other people's actions and decisions. Their leaving home is frequently not a real choice; it is necessary for physical and psychological survival. Every study or survey involving young homeless people confirms the significant percentage who leave home to escape physical and sexual violence.

Without a stable place to live, and no employment or schooling to go to, even the options for day-to-day activities are limited. Alder and Sandor (1989) refer to the 'daily dilemma' for young people of finding a safe place free from harassment when they are not able to stay in refuges and hostels during the day.

Physical and psychological health

In recent years, adolescent health has become an area of concern in Australia and it is recognised that services and approaches planned for adults are often not appropriate for a younger age group. While many adolescents have few health problems, for others it is a time of particular vulnerability. Rapid physical and sexual development, the prevalence in these years of certain illnesses such as asthma and diabetes, along with lack of access to reliable health information and feelings of being invulnerable make them susceptible.

The Burdekin Report devoted a chapter to health issues and established that psychological problems and poor physical health are major costs for young people who are homeless. The National Health and Medical Research Council (1991) believes that while in some ways the health needs of homeless young people are similar to the health needs of young people in general, there are special considerations with regard to the likely severity of their problems, their increased vulnerability and the way in which they interact with those providing health care. This report states that the majority of homeless youth have health problems; most have more than one problem.

The conditions under which young homeless people live make it difficult for them to look after themselves properly, and to take normal precautions against ill health. Poverty means often being hungry and cold and therefore more susceptible to illness and disease. Lack of money means that some services can't be afforded, and young people are often intimidated by, or alienated from, mainstream hospital services. What health education programs there are for adolescents have little or no hope of reaching homeless young people unless they are specifically designed to do so.

Some of the health problems which young homeless people commonly suffer from include poor nutrition, sleeping problems, poor physical and dental hygiene, skin infestations and infections; respiratory and gastrointestinal problems, sexually transmitted diseases, and eye and ear infections (Human Rights and Equal Opportunity Commission 1989, National Health and Medical Research Council 1991). Lack of preventive health care, such as regular PAP smears, increases the likelihood of problems going untreated; poor care of chronic illnesses such as asthma and diabetes increases suffering, and correctable problems such as poor eyesight go uncorrected. Sexual health is often poor as a result of sexual abuse and multiple sexual partners; drug use may lead to infertility.

As for psychological health, depression, insomnia, bulimia and anorexia are often problems, particularly for young women. About three-quarters of the females and 70 per cent of the males in a survey of homeless youth in inner-city Sydney said they did not like themselves much, and reported a number of behaviours which could indicate a degree of emotional stress or disturbance. Both females and males reported high levels of anger and anxiety, and difficulties in sleeping (Howard 1992).

The consequences of homelessness include low self-esteem, often further aggravated by the stress of instability and resulting in the development of entrenched psychological and behaviour problems, social isolation, and feelings of hopelessness. Anger about physical and sexual abuse together with low self-esteem and sense of powerlessness may lead to violence against others, suicide attempts and self-mutilation. Suicide attempts had been made by 82 per cent of the females and 61 per cent of the males in a group of inner-city Sydney young homeless people (Howard 1992). Most commonly, the attempts had been by drug overdose, but there was also a high degree of self-inflicted wounds to their bodies (over 66 per cent of both sexes).

A study in America indicated that protection against mental health problems in adolescents is related to a strong sense of connectedness with at least one caring adult, and to positive body image. Significant risk factors include a generalised fear of violence, a history of mental treatment in the family, high perceived use of alcohol and drugs at school, and the increased age of the adolescent (Resnick 1992). The favourable situation is almost the reverse of the circumstances of the majority of young people who are homeless. They frequently don't have the protective factors and do have the risk factors. They have often left home because for a variety of reasons the adults in their lives have been unable to care for them, and they are frequently reluctant to, or wary of, forming other attachments. On the other hand, violence and fear of violence, on the streets, in squats and from police, is a very common experience for young homeless people (Alder and Sandor 1989) and the violence of sexual assault has a devastating effect on the lives of many girls and young women (Robson 1992). Young homeless people are often seen as a group particularly at risk of heavy alcohol consumption and involvement with a range of other drugs.

It is difficult to get any clear idea of the proportion of young homeless people who are drug users, but evidence presented to the Burdekin Inquiry suggested that the majority were involved in drug use of some kind (Human Rights and Equal Opportunity Commission 1989). It is often difficult to avoid or drugs are embraced as a way of coping with problems. Cormack, Pols and Christie (1992) concluded from a review of several studies that homeless youth are a significant group for 'hazardous and harmful' alcohol consumption. This is of course dependent on whether they have the money to obtain alcohol.

Howard (1992) found that levels of drug use for both males and females in the Sydney inner-city homeless population were many times that of the average New South Wales adolescent as reported in routine secondary school surveys. Young women claimed greater usage of more drugs than young men, and use of more than one drug was the norm. Wanting to feel good and being bored were the two main reported reasons for drug use. Such reported reasons often cover severe pain and despair, sometimes the result of sexual abuse. Howard also found that sexual abuse and heavy use of drugs, especially via injection, were significantly associated. Much of the sexual abuse of young women is unreported, not recognised or acknowledged, or inadequately dealt with by adults, and remains a continuing emotional trauma (Robson 1992).

There is increasing recognition that young people are a vulnerable group in the spread of HIV infection. The general consensus of studies across different groups of adolescents who vary according to gender, social class and sexual behaviour is that while adolescent knowledge of AIDS is increasing, there are still serious gaps and that increased knowledge does not necessarily result in safe sex behaviour, for a variety of reasons (Rosenthal and Moore 1991; Sullivan 1992; Youth Research Centre 1991).

Young homeless people are included in groups especially at risk because of the relatively high proportion who are engaged in prostitution and/or intravenous drug use. Not feeling good about oneself and feeling powerless also tend to increase the likelihood of unsafe behaviour as some don't really care what happens to them. The study of inner-city homeless youth in Sydney showed that there had been some reduction in risk behaviour between 1989–90 and 1990–91 in the area of intravenous drug use and sex with paying partners. However, with non-paying partners, there was less use of contraception. In addition, levels of regular HIV testing were low. Despite reasonable knowledge of how the virus is spread, not a lot was known about possible symptoms and there were stereotypic ideas of those most at risk (Howard 1992). However, as Howard points out, in this regard the attitudes and behaviour of young homeless people are not very different from other young people, and indeed from many adults.

The costs of HIV infection to individuals, to those around them and to society hardly need to be spelt out.

Institutionalisation and imprisonment

Approaches to placing young people in protective and corrective institutions have gone through some significant changes in recent years and far fewer children are placed under the long-term care of the state. However, being homeless, and all that that may imply (being unsupported, living in poverty, being on the streets, involved in drug use, living in dangerous situations, stealing, squatting), increases the likelihood that young people will come to the notice of either legal or protective authorities. The potential personal costs are many. They include police harassment, a criminal record, imprisonment, further reduced opportunities for employment, increasing alienation and general lack of hope. Young people are often not well served by existing legal aid and community legal services (O'Connor and Tilbury 1985) and they find legal and court systems, including children's courts, alienating and difficult to understand (O'Connor 1990). The progression of some young people from early homelessness to long-term alienation via the juvenile justice system is not difficult to understand.

A review of personal costs

Young homeless people are robbed of opportunities to participate in aspects of life which other young people take for granted. The interaction of housing instability, poverty and lack of support in many ways excludes them from the mainstream of life. We have seen that homelessness reduces opportunities to participate in employment, education and training. Those who have lost connections with the structures of school, work and family are increasingly marginalised, and 'on the outside' of society. It is often very difficult to re-establish the connections.

Sinfield's comments on poverty are again relevant. He argues that denying people chances of contributing impoverishes them because their ability to participate in the daily routine of the majority and to share in its rewards is limited (Sinfield 1981). Young homeless people have limited opportunities to take part in activities and networks which form the fabric of everyday life, including recreational activities, supportive family relationships, and safe and reliable personal friendships. These are important at any stage of life, but for young people, they are a fundamental part of developing a sense of identity and of competence. Without support they lack many of the circumstances for healthy physical and psychological development and opportunities for choices which make for a potentially productive life. Options and opportunities for the future as well as for the present are severely limited.

Costs to Society

How do these costs to individuals translate into costs to society? Clearly something is wrong when we allow young people to become homeless, and then tolerate the continuation of this situation, through neglect, avoidance and inadequate allocation of resources. Homelessness is frequently portrayed as a personal problem and there is no doubt that individuals bear the brunt of it. But it is fundamentally a social problem, and therefore has a social cost of significant proportions. Homelessness results from the way in which social institutions, including the family and schools are organised, the way in which governments manage and allocate resources, and the way in which people through their governments and communities decide their priorities.

In simple terms, if we allow young people to become and remain homeless, we risk losing their potential contribution to communities and to the broader society. At stake is more than the loss of 'human capital' used in order to increase production or construct the 'clever country'. There is a much less tangible loss when some groups are marginalised and unable to take part fully. We miss out on people's potential to enhance the common good if their understandings, competencies and skills are not able to be developed, are not used or not valued.

We also lose their potential to contribute to social life through normal human interaction in the many roles most of us fulfil some time in our lives, as friends, neighbours, citizens, workers, sisters or brothers, sons or daughters. The alienation, isolation and poverty of homelessness severely restricts activities such as visiting, entertaining, telephoning, keeping in contact, going places with family and friends, giving and receiving presents, helping, talking with, being there for someone, all of which are part of the exercise of social roles and the maintenance of bonds which form the fabric of society.

Society as a whole is diminished when a significant minority lose faith in its structures and values, and become despairing, cynical and uncertain. It is hardly surprising that young people do become disillusioned when they are excluded not just from obtaining the 'bonuses' but also the necessitites. Even those who are most resilient and resourceful are likely to be dismayed facing situations such as those reported recently by the National Youth Coalition for Housing (1993). In the ACT, the waiting time for moving from refuges in some areas is four years for a one-bedroom unit and even bedsitter accommodation is very difficult to obtain. Some see so little hope for the future that they give up. The number of young homeless people who suicide, attempt suicide or inflict violence on themselves is of great concern, and surely tells us that there is something deeply wrong with our social institutions.

The cost to society of youth homelessness may be long term as well as immediate. If young people remain homeless for long periods, confidence, sense of self and positive connection to social structures are difficult to re-establish. Particularly if they have not been able to develop work skills, or have not had work experience, it is likely that they will not be able to rejoin the mainstream, their futures will indeed be 'foreclosed', and society will be the poorer from their exclusion.

The potential for increased crime and violence is probably more easily recognised as a social cost than is young people's inability to contribute to society in positive ways. Homelessness is seen as a threat to social order, because it breeds alienation and anger in young people who are excluded from the material benefits of society. It is certainly true that in most studies, some young people admit to stealing things and getting money and goods through illegal means because they are hungry and desperate; a significant number become users of illegal drugs; young homeless people are involved in violence on the streets. However, it is difficult and perhaps not very useful to estimate the amount of crime which occurs as a direct result of homelessness. It is also important not to operate on stereotypes about young homeless people being involved in crime, or to lump all crime and violence together. There are important distinctions to be made between stealing because you are hungry, and what seems to be gratuitous violence.

Rather than seeing increased crime as a cost of homelessness, we need to look to broader social causes of non-violent crime, and to aspects of Australian society and culture which makes violence so prevalent, particularly among males. The increased potential for young male violence in Australia, as in other industrialised societies, is likely to be a consequence of social and labour market changes which have closed off work opportunities with all that implies, producing an 'underclass'. Alder (1992) argues that research into the forms of violence which are on the increase supports the view that in societies where masculine identity is closely tied to work and economic independence, some males seek confirmation of their masculinity in other ways when they are excluded from work structures. Violence becomes a way to establish a sense of power, or to express anger at their deprivation. Young men at the lower end of the economic spectrum who have not had the chance to even begin a work career are particularly prone to such violence.

Having said this, it is also true that, regardless of what young people (homeless and not homeless) are actually doing, merely because they are on the streets and visible, they are often seen as a potential threat to social order (White 1990). In addition, young homeless people themselves are exploited, harassed, and the victims of a frightening degree of criminal violence. In their families, in youth refuges and on the streets, they are raped, assaulted and harassed (Alder and Sandor 1989; White, Underwood and Omelczuk 1991), sometimes by their age peers but very often by adults, including police.

A Better Future

Ensuring a better future for more young people and minimising the social costs outlined in this chapter require action on many fronts, including education, employment, income support, housing, health and family support programs. They also require involvement of local communities and individual citizens as well as commitment from governments, in terms of policy directions and adequate resources.

This book is about the very positive contribution which schools and their communities can make to the lives of young people who are homeless or at risk of being homeless. At present government policies are firmly aimed at increasing school participation and retention rates. A recent report recommended that by 2001, all but a minority of under-20-year-olds should have completed year 12 or an initial post-school qualification, or be participating in education or training(Australian Education Council 1991). However, for most young people who are homelessness and without adult support, remaining at school is all but impossible. They don't have the financial and personal resources to continue their education.

It might be argued that being able to stay at school is of questionable value in the present circumstances, where a significant proportion face the prospect of prolonged education with no job at the end of it. However, it is important that staying on at school or returning to school after an absence remains a real option for all young people. Access to education is a fundamental right with many potentially positive outcomes for individuals and society. Ideally, it provides the potential for a wider range of future options, introduces young people to ideas and interests they don't meet in their peer-group, provides skills and broadens personal horizons. Schools should therefore be resourced to provide educational programs and an environment appropriate to all young people. Previous chapters show how, with community support and adequate resources, schools can provide a range of practical assistance to help young people continue their schooling.

In addition to practical help, schools are well placed to be central community resources in tackling many of the issues discussed in this chapter. Schools are unique in their universality, their potential to cater for a range of ages, provide shared and individual learning experiences, combine education, recreation, personal development and social interaction, promote the involvement of parents and other adults, and be embedded in a community. They have considerable scope to help young people in a positive way through the development shifts referred to earlier.

School-based programs for young homeless people can contribute to a sense of attachment and connection for those who have become 'detached' from their families or from other safe and supportive networks. They can provide experiences of achievement and success for young people which enhance confidence and that positive sense of self, which has so often been dashed. Through a variety of means, they can provide young people with chances to contribute to their immediate and wider communities. In short, they can promote inclusion and participation, and counter the exclusion and alienation which is so often a part of being homeless. Both young people and society benefit.

Any society owes its young people the best possible opportunities to assume healthy and adult roles, both because the wellbeing of each individual is important in itself, and because of the potential contribution of individuals to the collective wellbeing. At risk if we do not do this are young people's lives, and their positive input to the common good now and in the future.

8

Economic Benefits of Supporting Homeless Young People

Homelessness, particularly that of young people, inflicts substantial economic costs on the community as well as personal costs on the individuals and families concerned. These economic costs are often overlooked in discussions about the problems of homelessness. But their significance is such as to justify policy action to deal with these problems even if governments and the community were to ignore all the arguments about social and personal costs set out in the previous chapter.

Put somewhat differently, the benefits of addressing and solving the problem of youth homelessness accrue to the community and the economy as well as to the particular individuals concerned. The benefits fall into two distinct categories: avoiding costs and outlays that are incurred because people are homeless (essentially a negative justification for action) and the more positive aspect of helping people contribute to the economic activity of the nation.

Both categories are extremely important. The short- and long-run costs of homeless people include substantial calls on federal, state and local government and voluntary sector funding in many areas. These include income support or social security outlays, the provision of housing, health and community services, calls on education, training and job search expenditures and calls on the policing, criminal justice and related areas.

To the extent that it is possible to reduce these outlays by reducing youth homelessness, the community and the national economy will benefit. This is so even when addressing the problems of youth homelessness itself involves substantial government outlays. In reality, the choice for the government is between spending money on damage control—meeting the costs directly resulting from youth homelessness—or on preventive measures to reduce the extent and resulting costs of homelessness.

In this specific context, the economic benefits to the nation of using all human resources, especially of young people, to best advantage takes on a very important dimension. Homeless people, with few exceptions, are people not attached to or participating in the workforce.

Instead of generating output and providing incomes, these people are reliant on private- and government-sector services to survive. The nation loses in two ways as a result, by reduced levels of national income and output and by no or reduced tax collections from the incomes of homeless people.

With the high and continuing levels of youth unemployment, it may be pointless to concentrate on the short-run benefits of increasing the number of young people able and willing to participate in the workforce. Indeed, many homeless young people have reached this state of affairs because of their inability to obtain paid employment.

Nevertheless, in the medium and longer term and even sometimes in the short term, addressing the problems of homelessness must assist the employability of young people who are presently homeless. The longer the period of unemployment and the more serious the personal position of the individuals concerned become, the less likely they are to be able to make a meaningful contribution to their own well-being and national output.

The remainder of this chapter concentrates on more specific details of the costs of youth homelessness, concluding with discussions of policy responses that may be able to help address current problems. Before this, one point is relevant. For the government to address the problems of youth homelessness, it is absolutely essential that the economy be operated on a basis that helps maximise employment opportunities and national income.

A healthy and properly functioning economy is a prerequisite to ensuring that all young (and older) people have a tangible opportunity to participate in the workforce. Without such an opportunity, many Australians, not confined to homeless people, will not be given a chance to participate in the workforce.

These and related issues are discussed in my recent Brotherhood of St Laurence research paper *Unemployment: The Economic and Social Costs* (Dixon 1992) where I argue that current high levels of unemployment could be costing the Australian economy as much as $18 billion annually. These costs are in addition to the immense private costs presently being borne by the unemployed and their families.

Consideration of Specific Issues

By far the most important economic costs of youth homelessness are the government support payments made to homeless young people. These payments are made either by way of Job Search Allowance (JSA) or special payments to Homeless Youth. The payments vary with the age of the recipient and their status. For example, homeless people with children can be eligible for the Sole Parent Pension which includes special supplements for children.

Homeless youth are eligible for an income support payment of around $210 per fortnight, with higher payments being available to older people and those with dependants. This payment in excess of $5000 per year per person has a very large cost to the community if paid for any extended period.

In the extreme and unfortunately increasingly possible case where youth homelessness results in continuing periods of unemployment into later life, a perpetual state of dependence on income-support payments, including sickness benefits, is a highly probable outcome.

Continuing dependence on income support for 20 years, for example from age 16 to age 40 with some brief periods in employment, would cost the community a minimum of $100 000 in income-support payments per person. Even if only

1000 people were to fall into this category, the long-run costs to the community of such an outcome would be a minimum of $100 million, expressed in terms of today's dollars.

The most serious and depressing aspect of such long periods on income-support payments is the associated loss in taxation revenue for the government. Compared with the situation where the young person is in paid employment and paying income tax and other taxes on their outlays, the costs of paying income-support payments are very large indeed.

On a taxable income of $17 000 a year, for example, tax of around $2300 a year is payable to the government increasing the total cost, including payment of income support, to in excess of $7400 a year in such a situation. In cases where wage incomes would be higher, the cost to the government of an unemployed homeless person would be higher, whereas for lower incomes, the loss in tax revenue would be a less significant factor.

The aggregate annual cost to the government depends, of course, on the total number of homeless people and their potential to earn income if unemployed. Even if the numbers of homeless people at any one time is only 10 000 people, the aggregate cost to the community would be $70 million annually—reason enough for the government to take the problem of homelessness seriously.

In assessing the significance of the above costs, the direct linkages between homelessness and unemployment are paramount considerations. For participation both in the education system and the labour market, having a place to live is a crucial requirement. Being homeless presents major difficulties for people wanting to participate on a regular basis in the workforce.

Even for part-time or casual employment, most employers want to be able to easily contact their employees as and when required. And even when such a point of contact is not required, the potential worker needs a place to be able to leave their personal effects while they are working.

Without a suitable home, the employability of young people is reduced also because of the problems of ensuring a clean and presentable appearance for dealing with customers and fellow workers. This is aside from the other problems discussed below associated with homelessness, including health, drug and alcohol problems.

In an economic environment of high and continuing levels of unemployment, any negative aspects associated with a job seeker will in almost all cases result in that person being passed over in favour of another job applicant. The fact that a person is homeless or has no fixed address will thus be a substantial handicap in any attempts to seek employment.

Associated with the lack of a home are other problems which include nutritional and related health problems, disrupted education (particularly for younger children), anti-social and criminal behaviour (if only to get enough income to survive) and drug and alcohol dependence. Even if the homeless young person is able to survive without engaging in criminal activities, many are forced into undesired and health-threatening sexual activities either to get money or to obtain temporary accommodation.

In terms of economic and social costs, all these problems involve the community in substantial actual or potential outlays, if only to alleviate and/or address actual or emerging problems to the community. The precise costs vary from situation to situation and individual to individual. In some cases also, the pressures are felt as an addition to the demands for scarce resources such as public hospital funding.

The economic costs to the community of a young homeless person who contracts the HIV virus and subsequently the AIDS infection are, for example, very substantial because of the costs of the medical and hospital services required to treat this illness. Work undertaken for the Burdekin Homeless Youth Inquiry uncovered, in one small group of homeless young people of Sydney's King's Cross area, a depressingly high incidence of HIV virus infection due to the sexual and drug-taking activities of the individuals concerned.

In addition to the costs of dealing with such health problems, the incidence of this disease and similar health problems virtually destroys any long-run hope of employability of the individuals affected. Health problems result in a continuing need for Commonwealth income-support payments either in the form of sickness benefit or in cases of more serious illness, disability support pension.

Young females, even when in a state of poor health, can gain access to the Sole Parent Pension when, as often happens, they bear a child outside a stable or de facto marriage relationship. When drug and alcohol dependence are involved, the probability of criminal behaviour in order to fund the dependence increases markedly.

The direct causal relationship between homelessness and criminal activity is a difficult one to demonstrate in all cases. But the need for money that cannot be met through employment obviously results in petty and even major criminal activities such as burglary, assault and related activities.

The community bears the costs from such activities in three separate ways. These are: first, the personal losses suffered by victims of the criminal activities; second, increased cost of insurance against theft via higher insurance premiums; and third, the costs to government and thus all taxpayers of policing and criminal justice activity.

Apart from the ongoing costs of the policing system, the specific costs of the criminal justice system, including those of the detention and jail facilities, are very large indeed. To keep a young person in detention, which is required all too frequently, requires a minimum annual budgetary outlay of at least $30 000 and more commonly as much as $50 000.

Once in the criminal justice system, homeless young people face considerable additional difficulties in returning to mainstream economic activities. Indeed, past experiences in detention centres, even as juvenile offenders, increases the probability of further offences later in life.

It is not possible to quantify, with reasonable precision, the actual costs in all of the above areas to the Australian community from youth homelessness. What is certain, however, is that the costs involved are sufficiently large to justify the highest possible priority being given to preventive action. Such action is, in any event, required on social justice grounds to help ensure that all Australians have access to affordable housing and the opportunity to participate in the labour force.

From the national viewpoint, such action is equivalent to an investment in human capital to maximise the potential of the individuals concerned to participate in the Australian economy. Experience has shown that with help and well-designed programs, homeless young people can be rehabilitated back into the community even if not into their family.

With the increasing incidence of marriage breakdown in the Australian community, the numbers of homeless young people coming from an unstable or non-existent family situation is increasing. This increases the need for the community to ensure that a network of services are available to young people facing personal difficulties, especially with obtaining affordable accommodation.

To the present time, not enough effort has been given to preventing and/or alleviating the problems associated with youth homelessness. However, the Burdekin Report and subsequent government initiatives have highlighted the potential benefits to both the community and the individuals concerned from action to dealt with the problems of youth homelessness.

Unfortunately, budgetary problems at all levels of government are constraining the funds that can be made available for individual social welfare programs, even the highest priority ones. This will complicate the task of those people pressing for immediate action to deal with youth and other homelessness.

One policy option warranting serious consideration is to integrate all the existing programs bearing upon homeless youth into the one funding allocation. Doing this would not obviate the need for additional budgetary outlays but it would make it possible to integrate income support, education and training and housing support programs into a coherent whole where attention can be paid to other issues such as health and drug dependence problems.

Benefits to the Community

The possibility of self-help programs, where young people are enlisted via education and training programs using money that in part would have to be spent on income-support programs, needs to be considered seriously. Enlisting the support of the voluntary and private sectors can also augment the available funding and equally importantly, open up the possibility of access to alternative support networks other than the young person's own family.

Regrettably, the case of homeless youth provides an excellent case-study of the substantial economic costs of specific social welfare programs. The mere fact of homelessness deprives the nation of the services of another employed worker and instead adds to the already large number of people in receipt of government income support and reliant on government-provided services for their well-being.

To the extent that individuals are helped and encouraged to provide for themselves in the longer term, any moneys spent are certain to provide substantial and tangible benefits to the community both in reduced calls on the budget and higher personal incomes with associated benefits to tax collections and reductions in government outlays.

The Education System

In the context of minimising long-run costs to the economy of youth homelessness, programs that assist or allow homeless children to remain in the education system are potentially very effective ones. The costs to the community and the economy are greatly increased if homelessness prevents children completing or continuing their education.

To be effective participants in the workforce, young people require successful education to obtain jobs in most areas. And even where a high level of educational achievement is not required, well-educated people are better placed to obtain whatever jobs are available.

Participation in the education system also helps the personal development of the individuals affected and can assist in finding suitable longer run housing for participants in the relevant program. In these ways, the economy will receive substantial benefits from such programs to assist homeless children to remain in the education system.

9

The School, Youth Homelessness and the Future

The first part of this book discusses the Ardoch program at Prahran Secondary College and illustrates the type of small-scale, local community-based action, which is necessary both to reduce youth homelessness and to prevent it.

Apart from its shining virtue in helping restore to a small number of young Australians a sense of hope and the probability of a continuing attachment to the life of the community from which they have been excluded, the Ardoch program contains important reminders for almost everyone else: policy makers, service providers, business people and general members of the Australian community.

These reminders are fivefold: first, that homeless young people are all individuals, not a homogenous category; second, that local programs developed by individuals and small groups can be ways of pricking the public conscience and encouraging the processes of reforms through pin-pointing the issues to be addressed by policies; third, that 'breaking the cycle' of youth homelessness must be simultaneously more complex and more continuous than simply locating a shelter or placing young people in refuges. Fourth, the Ardoch program challenges the current view among some service providers that by teenage years it is 'too late'; in other words that only early intervention (pre- or primary school) can be successful. Fifth, the Ardoch program asserts that not only can some young people be rescued from chronic homelessness through an educational program, but that a school can actively prevent *other* young people becoming homeless.

The purpose of this chapter is to discuss the aspects outlined above of the Ardoch program and in doing so, to provide an agenda for further development in this field for both programs and policies. Those of us working in this area are at times disheartened by apparently slow progress and at the adverse impact of 'externalities' on reform (such as Australia's poor economic performance) and consequent budget reductions (Carter 1993). But we need to remember that the recognition by federal and state governments of the incidence and experience of homelessness, that government efforts to commit at least some new resources to the area, that the increased access of homeless young people to income security, are major advances when comparing Australia with the lack of official recognition and resources in the United Kingdom and the United States of America. In addition, since the National Inquiry into Homeless Children reported in 1989 (Human Rights and Equal Opportunity Commission 1989), there has been a marked advance in public understanding and goodwill about youth homelessness, assisted by responsive media. While the imbalance between resource demand and supply is serious, it is also true that new forms of philanthropy have been defined, as some communities, churches and businesses delineate their social responsibilities as sharing their financial and other profits by investing in the homeless young people in the communities in which they operate.

Homeless Young People are Individuals

To deal with the first reminder, that homeless young people are individuals, not a category, means that the Ardoch program has challenged two communal myths about homeless young people. The first is that youth homelessness is a romantic state. By objectifying the 'street kid' as the essence of 1990s counter-culture, the fashion magazine *Mode* says:

> She's crumpled and smudged, unlike the pure-as-driven snow gamines of yester-year, who, although pert and feisty, seemed

to be hopelessly naive ... The dictionary definition of gamin(e) means: ' a neglected and unruly child in the streets', a sweet little girl who happens to be in a sweet little mess with tangled hair and shredded clothes and vegemite on her mouth ... Fashion 1993 style is ... grunge and gamine. Fashion has at last embraced the street people—the new gamine is more likely to have spent the night in a dump truck than in Jean-Paul Belmondo's bed. (Tulloch 1993: 18)

On this reading, the street kid is the descendant of the 1960s hippy, a volunteer outsider and critic of mainstream society; an alternative lifestyler and utopian romantic who seeks and deserves privileged status as simultaneous prophet and consumer of contemporary capitalism. The *raison d'être* of the 1960s and 1970s 'hippy' withdrawal was centred on the non-essentiality of the work ethic and the rejection of the nuclear family. Thus, by association, it is assumed that street life is a chosen form of 'agit prop' and a reaction against conformity. As the accounts of this book make clear, the ascription of the 'street-kid-as-hero' is far from adequate. Far from living a satisfying, self-sufficient life, rejecting labour and family norms from the fringe of mainstream society, many homeless young people are victims of the unpleasant excesses of capitalism—drug dealers, unscrupulous employers and exploitative landlords. The nights in the dump truck or the Brotherhood bin, or in temporary sale of the body to an unknown adult, are no compensation for the loss of attachments of family, school and work.

The other myth which deals with youth homelessness as a category is to view all homeless young people as 'bludgers', as illegitimate drains on an overtaxed welfare system. When the report of the National Inquiry into Youth Homelessness was published in 1989 (Human Rights and Equal Opportunity Commission 1989), the privately expressed opinions of some members of the federal ministry gave credence to this view. At the time, the federal government was attempting to reduce the numbers of people on the social security rolls (Saunders 1990; Carter 1993). A massive operation against fraud was taking place and, in addition, there were restrictions on the access of young people (especially 16–18-year-olds) to the social security system.

The deliberate construction of new claims of eligibility for entry to the social security system threatened the government imperative of reducing public expenditures. An analysis of ministerial responses to the release of the Inquiry report about the needs of homeless young people included the following reactions.

Rationalisation—'Youth homelessness is purely seasonal' (i.e., young people will work in the winter but arrange to be off work in summer and seek benefits).

Suppression—'Youth homelessness is rare and confined to a few trouble spots in the "bright lights" (such as Kings Cross and St Kilda). It has been "talked up" and vastly overdramatised by the Commissioners.'

Concealment—'If we [the government] lie low, the Inquiry report will be a four-week-wonder: the Commissioners will soon become tired and go away.'

Conspiracy—'Youth homelessness is the product of youth workers who refuse to return young people to their families. The Commissioners have been "captured" by vested interests who build up and maintain the numbers of young homeless people, at the expense of returning them to the families where they belong.'

Each of these political defences (rationalisation, suppression, concealment and conspiracy) was based on the notion that any possible legitimacy of a young homeless person's additional claim on the welfare system, either by right or by need, had to be denied or discredited. Thus to maintain the barrier against a claim, the homogeneity of the category 'homeless young people' needed to be preserved. The common characteristic of the group was seen to be its work-shy nature: a category which, by definition, would prefer to be surfing than working. The evasion of the work ethic and work habit and the attendant threat to the public order that this group posed was a stereotype which informed the development of public policy. In 1993 it is still necessary to deal with versions of the two stereotypes outlined above without disagreeing that there may well be a minority of individuals for whom either stereotype might be accurate.

Community Initiatives and Human Rights

The second reminder given us by the Ardoch program is that individual or community action need not await government imprimatur, or even sponsorship. Compared with its response in the 1960s and 1970s, the Commonwealth Government looked less favourably on the small, grass-roots community-based experiments, at least in the 1980s. Programs developed from policies developed in Canberra, and were delivered 'top down', sometimes on to unsuspecting or bemused local communities. The origins of this 'policy correctness' was, in part, the desire to reduce government expenditure and indeed in the later half of the 1980s, education, housing and social security allocations were reduced ostensibly to balance the federal budget, but under the supervision of economic theorists convinced that smaller government and less welfare would benefit the community by avoiding the evils of 'welfare dependency' (Pusey 1991).

Ironically while the federal government was reducing expenditure to the levels of the 1950s, other areas of government were implicitly expanding remits by committing Australia to the implementation of international policies on human rights for children and young people. As this chapter will later discuss, it was the members of schools, businesses and local churches who responded to youth homelessness and who, unwittingly, were responding to the spirit of the United Nations Convention on the Rights of the Child, by providing shelter, income, a decent education, protection and friendship. Probably unbeknownst to the federal Treasury, in 1991, Australia, a signatory to the United Nations Convention on the Rights of the Child, guaranteed its children and young people the right to 'equal access to secondary and higher education, directed at developing ... personality and talents to the fullest potential' (Articles 28 and 29). If a child or young person was deprived of a family environment, whether temporarily or permanently, he or she was now 'entitled to special protection and assistance from the State' (Articles 20, 21, 25). In addition, a child or a young person gained the right to 'benefit from social security and to an adequate standard ... of living', particularly with regard to nutrition, clothing and housing (Articles 26 and 27). As well, the child aquired the right to 'protection from all forms of physical, sexual or mental abuse . . . and to the promotion of his or her physical and psychological recovery from abuse, neglect and exploitation' (Articles 18, 19, 32–36, 39) (Brewer and Swain 1993).

For many thousands of homeless Australian children and young people, the fact that their government has guaranteed these rights will be surprisingly good news. But in reality, a recent report, a critique of Australia's compliance with the United Nations Convention of the Rights of the Child, notes that there are clear breaches of the Convention, which constitute both severe abuses of human rights and major omissions of duty. These omissions stem from, first, ignorance about the Convention from those who ought to know about it and second, failure by the government to develop and resource children's services adequately (Brewer and Swain 1993).

Viewed from this angle, and given the purposive reductions in federal expenditure, the first part of this book implies that a range of basic human rights of many of Australia's young people are being taken-for-granted, or overlooked, violated and systematically abused. Those few homeless young people fortunate enough to be included in the Ardoch or another program which acknowledges the claims of young people to an adequate education, income, housing, and protection are a favoured few. The hand-to-mouth nature of the Ardoch program, its imbalance between demand and supply, are testament to the durability and conviction of its staff and key supporters.

Housing Alone is Not the Solution

The third orthodoxy that the Ardoch program challenges is the belief that housing is the single solution to youth homelessness, a view repeated often in the Australian and international literature. 'The cause of homelessness is lack of housing' (Kozol 1988: 11). When 'solutions' to social problems are 'captured' by interest groups, the interlocking nature of social problems is often obscured. For example, when the mental hospitals were decanted in the USA and the United Kingdom in the 1970s, in the cause of deinstitutionalisation, it was assumed (because the medical profession said so) that the major need of severely and chronically mentally ill patients discharged to the community was for effective *treatment* programs. In fact, in retrospect, the prior need was for stable, affordable, housing. As a result, the homeless mentally ill swelled the street population in major US and UK cities. In Australia, Anne Deveson's personal account of her homeless mentally ill son, Jonathon (Deveson 1991), on the streets of Sydney and Adelaide and Herrman's research of mental illness in the homeless population of Melbourne (Herrman 1990) confirms that far too few sheltered housing options were established and that appropriate connections to services for income, education, training and jobs were not made.

Intuitively, the Ardoch program recognised that the provision of accommodation was not on its own a solution. In its insistence that a range of objectives be addressed either simultaneously or in sequence, according to the young person's need, the Ardoch program was ahead of its time. In providing material resources (housing, food, clothing, sanitation); opening up the opportunity to link to a universally used institution (the school) and thus to the acceptable role of student; recognising the need for social support and an affectional relationship which reflects personal worth, the Ardoch program demonstrated both the possibilities and the limitations.

Most children and young people grow up through and by attachment to two universal institutions, the family and the school. Thus, one important strategy is to reinstitute connections wherever possible between the two key institutions, family and school, and the young person. The connection with family may not be literal; reuniting with parents may not be possible or politic, and a substitute family, or even a 'family' of peers may need to be found. Likewise, unless a young person is reconnected to 'education' in its broadest sense—through a secondary school, an apprenticeship, a traineeship or even on-the-job-training—the connection between the homeless young person and a role in the community will not be achieved.

Adolescence is Not Too Late

Fourth, the Ardoch experience challenges the views of some welfare agencies that it is not worth investing in youth programs, because it is 'too late'. In concert with the Jesuits, 'give me a child until he is seven and I will show you the man', an overly deterministic and pessimistic view of human nature can refuse to acknowledge that young people can be more than contained or suppressed. Research has suggested that up to a half of homeless young people in Australia are ex or current wards of state. They are discharged from care with no concrete plans for income, housing, friends; almost no welfare organisation, government or non-government, has programs or plans to follow up young people after their discharge from care (Taylor 1990). Many large non-government agencies closed down their youth programs from the mid-1970s and the vacuum was filled by small, single-issue youth accommodation services, characterised by high staff turnover and isolation from other services in the community. Large church-based agencies have made amends since the publication of the National Inquiry Report (Human Rights and Equal Opportunity Commission 1989) and encouraged the development of local, sometimes parish-based, programs. The best of these recognise the range of material needs of young people and their needs for human relationships and affiliation. But in general, the pattern of services dependent on single-focus youth refuges has not changed since 1989 (Davis 1993).

Reaching young people (homeless or not) is not easy. Many reject authoritarian structures and all have been influenced by the internationalisation of communications, entertainment and fashion. Method and style are at least as important as content. As the earlier quotation from *Mode* magazine indicates (Tulloch 1993), homeless young people are not naive and the authenticity and genuineness of the helper is of more relevance to the homeless young person than other credentials such as age and formal qualifications. 'Open' situations are required to demonstrate this. Thus at Prahran Secondary College, as an accessory to classes, the breakfast program offers free movement, freedom of speech, equality between helper and student and peer support between homeless and non-homeless students.

The Ardoch program has been developed in the face of an awkward history of rejection of the welfare component of school programs by some education officials. But the stories of the young people themselves reflects that welfare itself has been fragmented, incoherent and discontinuous and often did little to provide sensitive and timely help to homeless young people. The chaotic shuttle through unrelated services and the isolation of many youth refuges mirrored the fragmentation, lack of continuity and dislocation within the young people's lives.

Some educators feel that to accept welfare programs for homeless students is to ask schools to do too much. There is a current argument that 'schools should educate' and that programs addressing socio-economic need should be handled by welfare agencies, not schools. This is understandable, but if schools are to take student achievement seriously, the mission of the school needs to be dual—the academic development of students and their general development as human beings. As Comer argues,

> The nature of neighbourhoods during the agricultural and early and middle industrial periods made this dual focus natural for many schools. Fellow feeling, or community, could exist even when there was unfairness and abuse of various groups. When neighbourhoods changed because of technological advance in transportation, communication and other areas, schools failed to adjust and as a result, failed to meet the needs of many students, particularly low income and minority students. (Comer 1986: 208–9)

Comer concludes that it is possible to provide a good education for students at all socio-economic levels and to make a school an important part of the interest and effort of local communities, provided there is consistent and equitable financial support, improved in-service preparation of staff and changes in organisation and management which emphasise diagnostic and creative teaching, making students responsible for their own learning and the promotion of higher order thinking through team-teaching, time-block scheduling and open classrooms.

Certainly schools cannot be expected to take over where the welfare agency has failed. But for those homeless young people who decide voluntarily to reconnect with school, a comprehensive support program can help to compensate for the past failures of family, and welfare. Further, a school program is more likely to be able to offer training in citizenship to a young person than a stand alone welfare program. At the Ardoch program, the notion of obligation to others is developed through a range of methods, including having young people raise money for the program, come back to school after departure as mentors, and so on. The issue of obligation as opposed to entitlement is central to all current debates about welfare policies. But at a human level, it is clear that there need be no conflict between meeting entitlements and encouraging responsibility to others. It is perhaps a pity that it has been left to the most conservative welfare theorists of the New Right to polarise issues of entitlement and obligation. Projects such as Ardoch suggest that the two issues can be treated as the two sides of the one coin, that an effective model of citizenship can be communicated and demonstrated.

The Prevention of Youth Homelessness

Fifth, the Ardoch program signals that youth homelessness needs to be prevented. As definitions of homelessness within this book indicate, many young people, if not literally living on the streets, are on the verge of homelessness and lack a home. As a 'universal' institution, schools are in a critical position to prevent further homelessness. If a young person leaves his or her family, the aim should be assist him or her to stay at school. Likewise, a young person who leaves school needs to be supported by a family. Without either form of support, a young person's chances of becoming at least temporarily homeless are increased.

Support for vulnerable families is an essential part of prevention. Parents of younger children now have many more supports than in the recent past, say twenty-five years ago, with a range of income security supports such as the family allowance supplement and sole parent's pension available, and child-care services and even playgroups have improved the quality of life of many parents of young children. For many families who are vulnerable to poverty, isolation or other disadvantage through unemployment, high housing costs, low wages, inadequate benefits or sole parenthood (Harris 1989), adolescence exacerbates stresses which have been dormant during earlier years. But the expectation is that families (including sole parents) should be able to cope in a self-contained fashion, and requests for support are identified as failure; despite the known confusion and difficulties that adolescent life raise for families.

School-based preventative programs can offer financial, material and housing assistance to vulnerable families. It will bring families together to assist them to understand their own needs, and the needs of their young people as they make the transition to adulthood. The need for support must not be identified as family failure. The aim of a preventative program is not necessarily to keep young people living with their parents, but to ensure that, first, young people can remain in their families for so long as it is appropriate and safe for them to do so and, second, when they do leave home, they can maintain good family relations. The problem is not that young people leave home, but when and how they do so (Boyce, Carter and Elkington 1991).

A preventative program must therefore aim to strengthen the attachment and links of young people to their local community, and particularly to adults outside their family of origin. The aim is to provide a school community where young people have a place of value in their own right rather than this being linked to money, possessions, alcohol or drugs.

The risk factors being dealt with by a prevention program are inadequate income, lack of housing, early school leaving, unemployment, high levels of family conflict and poor links with the local community. These in combination with changing social values place young people at risk of homelessness. These risk factors have emerged as a result of changes in Australian society over the past twenty-five years. It is the interrelationship between them, rather than any one factor, which leads to homelessness. Thus early leaving of either the school or the family is not new, but has now become a significant risk factor because of youth unemployment and family breakdown. It is very important therefore in a prevention program that these issues are not addressed in isolation from each other (Boyce, Carter and Elkington 1991).

Social scientists have been more adept at defining the risk factors (unemployment, lack of income, housing, family breakdown, etc.) than the factors which *protect* against youth homelessness. We can conceive of *protective* factors as the other side of the coin to the risk factors. Resources (adequate income, housing, education, employment) and relationships (stable family life and involvement in the local community) are the elements which provide *protection* against youth homelessness. Prevention needs to aim at maintaining or rebuilding young people's attachments by increasing the level of protective factors, thereby decreasing the risk factors.

The advantage of this approach is that it does not define the form that attachments should take for any young person. Thus to take an extreme example, a young person without significant family relationships and not living at home may be protected from youth homelessness and is not necessarily at high risk of homelessness if his or her other attachments are stable: for example, if he or she continues to attend school, he or she has an income and a relationship with other caring adults, say in a local church. Prevention in a school environment needs to aim at building up attachments to increase the protective factors in young people's lives (Boyce, Carter and Elkington 1991).

Within this framework, *primary prevention* involves addressing the underlying political, economic and social causes (local, state and national) which place young people at risk of homelessness. *Secondary prevention* involves identifying the young people in a school who are at most risk of homelessness. It involves strengthening their attachments by building up their protective factors, and decreasing their risk factors to ensure they do not become homeless. *Tertiary prevention* involves ensuring that young people who experience short periods of homelessness do not become chronically homeless. Any school must anticipate that some young people will experience brief periods of homelessness. It is important to resource and support these young people without relying on existing services for homeless young people, which are often more appropriate to the chronically homeless.

It is at the fourth level or *quaternary prevention* that most services for young homeless people are concentrated (for example, youth refuges). It is important that the concept of prevention is not abandoned even for young people who are chronically homeless. In such situations it is critical that a young person is not forsaken or allowed to disappear. The aim is to prevent permanent life long homelessness (Boyce, Carter and Elkington 1991).

The Politics of Hope

If there is a 'message' in the Ardoch program for the community at large, it concerns the politics of hope. The history of social reform suggests that it is a spirit of optimism and confidence which unlocks the door to constructive social improvements. Thus, the first reason for the significance of the Ardoch program is that it offers a faith in the future; in the empowerment of extremely disadvantaged young people whom society generally and the welfare system in particular would, by their collusive neglect, write off.

Exactly a century ago, in the early 1890s, Victoria suffered a catastrophic depression. All sections of the community suffered extreme poverty, hardship, illness and mortality. The social and economic disruption of the period was extreme; yet during this period, hope in the development of an egalitarian Australian nation was a thread running through the pain: a determination that this new country would surmount the grosser inequalities of the Old World. While no study exists on the specific fates of young people during this period, it can be safely assumed that despite the devastation of homelessness, unemployment and disease, for those children and young people who survived, the new century offered unparalleled opportunities. In the early years of the twentieth century, Australia's comparative wealth allowed it to develop unique forms of social protection—full employment, award wages, protectionism. Then it was possible for a homeless young person, without either a family or a good education to support him or herself. Indeed, many working-class families expected their young to leave home to find a job to support the family. Albert Facey was sent away from his grandmother's home at the age of 8 to a farm job where he was treated with great cruelty. He was unusually young, but from the age of 12, illiterate and unschooled, he supported himself within the workforce (Facey 1981).

A century ago, young people who survived the depression were offered a set of direct economic and social opportunities which may be denied the young people of the 1990s depression.

A hundred years ago, if a child survived the morbidity of childhood, he or she could anticipate a self-supporting economic future, whatever his or her level of education. But for the young people today, their life chances will reside in the trade off between the quantity and quality of their educational experience and levels of unemployment. A changed labour market, de-emphasising primary and manufacturing industries and emphasising service and information industries, has changed the shape of job prospects of all young people. If the quantity and quality of education is interrupted or discontinued, this increases the chances of joining the slow moving queue of the long-term unemployed.

Changes in the amount and type of work started a great deal earlier for young people than the recession of 1990. The demand for youth labour declined from the mid-1960s as the number of teenage jobs declined. Teenage jobs fell by a third between 1966 and 1988 (25 per cent for males and 39 per cent for females) (ABS 1992).

The federal government response to youth unemployment in the 1980s was to extend participation rates in education (by encouraging the completion of secondary education and expanding the tertiary system) and to withdraw benefits for the under-18s, by reducing the level of benefits for 16–18-year-olds and restricting their entitlement. The assumption was that young people participated in full time education until the age of 18 and were the responsibility of their parents, or else they were self supporting members of the workforce. The group sacrificed between these twin policies were young people not at school and without family support. The unintended consequence of the policy changes of 1987 were, in sequence, first: the growth of youth homelessness as young people were excluded from both unemployment benefit and employment; second, the return of some homeless young people to school, in search of an income (AUSTUDY) and, in some cases, a good education. It has been left to schools like Prahran Secondary College to pick up these casualties of altered labour-market conditions and changed social security entitlements, and to cope as best they can.

The emphasis of Ardoch and other school programs to date has been on the conditions needed to provide access to education for homeless young people and to answer the question:

what material resources and personal support do young people need to re-attach themselves to school?

But a further question is much more difficult. Once at school, what particular curriculum or program should each young person follow in order to improve his or her eventual chances of competing on the labour market for a job? There have been outstanding successes, at Ardoch, but, as with any program, there have also been failures. The way that any program, educational or social, deals with its less-than-brilliant prospects (those who are not high achievers) should be evaluated. Any business, school, health or welfare program needs to account for its wastage as well as for its successes.

But to return to the 1890s depression. If they did not die from typhoid or malnutrition, or emigrate, for example, to the goldfields of Western Australia, many children and young people turned to living on the streets, to prostitution and crime. Some were described as 'running about Melbourne, like dogs in Constantinople, cared for by no one, fed by no one, kicked by everybody' (Kennedy 1982: 213). Some fiction of the 1890s also describes the circumstances of young people: for example, Tasma (Jessie Couvreur), a woman writer, tells the compelling short story about M. Calouche, the homeless young boy taken on by a brutal employer, who drove the youngster literally to death. In death it was discovered that this frail boy was actually a girl (Tasma 1890). Then in 1893, the Reverend Horace Tucker, father of the founder of the Brotherhood of St Laurence, wrote a splendid utopian novel in which homeless young people of both sexes were rescued from the polluted, dangerous and unsympathetic streets of Melbourne for rehabilitation in an idyllic rural commune, where liberty, equality and fraternity flourished: a sense of belonging, a place in a community, education, meaningful work, beautiful surroundings, attractive housing, good fresh food, leisure rights, spiritual development and rights for women! (Tucker 1893).

Tucker's schemes for the abolition of poverty and homelessness may have been utopian but some features would not be out of place today. The emphasis on material resources, an optimistic ethos, and a role for all resonate with the findings of detailed research on services for homeless people today. Thus the key questions for the future are not now those concerning the range of *needs*, of homeless people, but questions about the *generation* and *distribution* of resources and the *modes* of program delivery.

The first issue, the generation and distribution of resources, has to be the fundamental question for the 1990s. More and more, the community as well as government will be attempting to discover new resource bases for their work. The experience of the 1960s and 1970s was that offering finance alone did not solve a problem, but poorly resourced services are not efficient or effective either. The key to the future for young homeless people, as for many other disadvantaged groups in the Australian community depends on our capacity to generate and maintain new jobs. All who are interested in reducing youth homelessness must turn their attention to job generation and to policies of full employment (Crossley 1991).

The second issue, the mode of service provision, is as important as the first. Services which do not empower their users to live co-operative, democratic lives in the community may do more harm than good in the long run. It is at the level of provision of services that models of citizenship and community can be lived out. This will involve a serious look at the philosophy of service provision and a recognition that empowerment and reciprocal obligation can flourish together. If this happens, other services for homeless young people can capture the imagination of the community as the Ardoch program has done, to the enrichment of all.

Bibliography

Alder, C. (1992) 'Violence, gender and social change', *International Social Science Journal*, 44(2): 268–75.
Alder, C. and Sandor, D. (1989) *Homeless youth as victims of violence*. Criminology Department, University of Melbourne.
Allatt, P. and Yeandle, S. (1992) *Youth Unemployment and the Family: voices of disordered times*. Routledge, London.
Amato, P. (1985) 'Growing Pains', *Australian Society*, (September): 6–10.
Attridge, M. (1992) Open the door: Independent Young People and Housing in Australia. A paper prepared for the National Housing Strategy. Australian Government Publishing Service, Canberra.
Australian Bureau of Statistics (ABS) (1992) Student Finances, Australia (1991) Cat.No. 6550.0 (ABS).
Australian Education Council. Review Committee (1991) *Young people's participation in post-compulsory education and training* (Finn Report). Australian Government Publishing Service, Canberra.
Barclay, L., Johns, L., Kennedy, P. and Power, K. (1991) Speaking of Housing . . . A report on a Consultation with Victorian women on Housing'. The Ministerial Advisory Committee on Women and Housing and Women in Supportive Housing (WISH), Melbourne.
Barrett, A. (1987) The HYPO Recipe: Documentation and Evaluation of the Housing and Young People's Outreach Service. Department of Community Services and Health, IYSH Focal Point Australia, Canberra.
Beed, C. (ed.) (1991) *What we need as home: cohesion of home as perceived by homeless youth*. A report from the Homelessness Research Team. Scripture Union, Victoria.
Boyce, J. (1991) *Out of Work, Out of Home*. Report of the Action Research Project, Unemployment and Youth Homelessness. Brotherhood of St Laurence, Melbourne, August.
——(1992) 'Youth exclusion and changing values', *Parity*, 5 (3): 8–9.

Boyce, J., Carter, J. and Elkington, D. (1991) The Prevention of Youth Homelessness. Unpublished paper.

Breen, K.(1987) 'Our Biggest Export Business is Kids': The Urban Accommodation Needs of Country Young People. Victorian Youth Policy Developmental Council and the Youth Accommodation Coalition of Victoria, February.

Brewer, G. and Swain, P. (1993) Where Rights are Wronged: A Critique of Australia's Compliance with the United Nations Convention on the Rights of the Child. National Children's Bureau.

Cahill, D. and Ewen, J. (1992) Youth in the wilderness: young people and the Commonwealth Government's Access and Equity Strategy. Unpublished manuscript, Phillip Institute of Technology, Melbourne.

Cairns Committee for Homeless Persons (1979) Cairns Homeless Persons Survey, June.

Carter, J. (1990) 'Urban Poverty as it affects children: some costs of child and youth homelessness', in Nixon, J., McWhirter, W., and Pearn, J. (eds), *Poverty in Childhood.* Amphion Press.

—— (1991) 'The Relevance of the Convention to Specific Concerns: Child and Family Welfare', in Alston, P. and Brennan, G. (eds), *The U.N. Children's Convention and Australia.* Human Rights and Equal Opportunity Commission, Australian National University Centre for International and Public Law and Australian Council of Social Service.

—— (1993) 'Dealing with Policy Failure', in Marsh, I. (ed.) *Governing in the Nineties.* Longman Cheshire, Melbourne.

Chamberlain, C., Mackenzie, D. and Brown, H. (1992) 'Understanding Contemporary Homelessness: Issues of Definition and Meaning', *Australian Journal of Social Issues,* 27 (4) (November): 274–97.

Chappell, C. (1980) *Youth Housing: Survey Report and Conference Proceedings.* SA Council of Social Service, Adelaide.

Chapman, B. and Smith, P. (1992) 'Predicting the long-term unemployed: a primer for the Commonwealth Employment Service', in Gregory, R. and Karmel, T. (eds), *Youth in the eighties, papers from the Australian Longitudinal Survey Research Project.* Department of Employment Education and Training and Centre for Economic Policy Research, Australian National University, Canberra.

Chesterman, C. (1988) *Homes Away From Home: Supported Accommodation Assistance Program.* Final Report of the National Review of the Supported Accommodation Assistance Program, January.

Coffey, M. and Wadelton, D. (1991) *Shelter and the Streets.* Youth Accommodation Association (NSW) Ltd, Sydney.

Comer, J. (1986) 'Education for Community', in Schorr, A. *Common Decency: Domestic Policies after Reagan.* Yale University Press.

Community Services Victoria (1991) *Victorian SAAP Client Data Collection Annual Report July 1990–June 1991.* Community Services Victoria, Melbourne.

Bibliography 147

Cormack, S., Pols, R. and Christie, P. (1992) 'Alcohol and drug use', in Kosky, R. Eshkevari, H. S. and Kneebone, G., *Challenges in adolescent mental health in Australia*. Australian Government Publishing Service, Canberra.

Council of Social Service of Tasmania (1979) The Results of a Survey into the Needs for the Provision of Accommodation Facilities for Young People, Undertaken by a Concerned Group of Tasmanian Organisations, June.

Crossley, L. (1990) *Children and the Future of Work*. Brotherhood of St Laurence, Melbourne.

Cummins, M. and Wilson, J. (1977) Accommodation Needs of Adolescents, Tasmania, November.

Cunnew, D. and Downie, M. (1986) New Directions for Housing Young People, Presentation of the South Australian Housing Trust to the Honourable The Minister of Housing and Construction.

Davis, N. (1993) 'Little Hope for the Young Homeless', *Australian*, 14 April.

Davison, G. (1978) *The Rise and Fall of Marvellous Melbourne*. Melbourne University Press.

Department of Employment, Education and Training, (1992), The Job Report, 1,1, October.

Department of Health, Housing, & Community Services, (1992) *New Services for homeless youth. A Federal/State response to youth homelessness*. Australian Government Publishing Service, Canberra.

Deveson, A. (1991) *Tell Me I'm Here*. Penguin, Melbourne.

de Vries, J. and Tunnell, A. (1990) The Employment, Education and Training Needs of Young People in Supported Accommodation. Youth Accommodation Coalition of Western Australia, Perth.

Dixon, D. (1992) *Unemployment: the Economic and Social Costs*. Brotherhood of St Laurence, Melbourne:

Duffield, B., Elliott, M. and Fall, M. (1979) A Survey into the Need for Emergency Accommodation in Townsville. Department of Community Welfare, Townsville College of Advanced Education, June.

Dwyer, P. (1989) 'A Summary and Analysis of the Burdekin Report', in Allison S. and Brownell, M. *Responses to Burdekin, Selected Responses to Our Homeless Youth*. National Clearinghouse for Youth Studies, Hobart, Tasmania.

Econsult Management Consultants, (1992a) Women's Access to the Private Rental Market. Draft report, for the Ministerial Advisory Committee on Women and Housing, Carlton, Victoria.

—— (1992b) SAAP Review and Planning Project. Issues Paper. Econsult (Australia) Pty Ltd, Melbourne.

Edgar, D. (1985) Family Conflict and Youth Outcomes. Barton Pope Memorial Lecture. South Australian Association for Mental Health, Adelaide, 25 September.

Facey, A. (1981) *A Fortunate Life*. Penguin, Melbourne.

Fopp, R. (1981) 'Submission' to the Senate Standing Committee Re Youth Homelessness, Senate: Official Hansard Report, Tuesday 8 December, 3531–51j.
—— (1987) Public Housing for Young People: A Review of Issues Researched, for the Office of Youth Affairs, Department of Prime Minister and Cabinet under the National Youth Affairs Research Scheme, June.
—— (1988) Estimating Young People in Australia: Estimating Numbers and Incidence, a Report for the Human Rights Commissioner, May 1988.
—— (1989a) Homeless in the City: The Report of the Review of Inner-City Services for Homeless Men. SAAP Unit, Department for Community Welfare, Adelaide.
—— (1989b) Public Housing for Young People: A Review of Issues Researched: A Position Paper. National Youth Affairs Research Scheme, Commonwealth Youth Bureau, Canberra.
—— (1991) Where From and Where To? Presented to the Housing Rights or Homeless Nights Conference, Melbourne, 10–13 October.
—— (1992a) Breaking the Cycle of Youth Homelessness, A report to the Council of Capital City Lord Mayors.
—— (1992b) 'Homelessness and Young People, Ranking Causes and Explanations', *Shelter—National Housing Action*, 8 (2) (Winter): 26–30.
—— (1992c) Homelessness: Implications for State Housing Authorities, a report for the Victorian Ministerial Advisory Committee on Homelessness and Housing, Melbourne, September.
Fopp and Ellis, B., Rogers, R. and Williams, J. (1990) Accommodating a Second Go: Determination, Commitment and Assistance, A study into the accommodation and housing needs of selected students from the Elizabeth West Re-entry School, Umbrella Youth Housing Association, September.
Ford, P. (1988) Women's Emergency Services Program: Working Paper, SAAP Review, January.
Gardiner, K. and O'Neil, M. (1987) 'What Are Nice Girls Like You Doing In A Place Like This?' A Report on Young Women's Access to Youth Housing, National Youth Coalition for Housing, December.
Harris, P. (1989) *Child Poverty, Inequality and Social Justice*. Brotherhood of St Laurence, Melbourne.
Hart, A. (1979) Survey of Homeless Persons in Perth. DSS, Perth.
Hartley, R. (1990) 'The Never Empty Nest', *Family Matters*, 26 (August): 67–9.
—— (1991) what young adults rate as important, *Family Matters*, 29 (August): 28–31.
—— (1992) unpublished data from the Becoming Adult Study, Australian Institute of Family Studies, Melbourne.
Herrman, H., McGorry, P., Bennett, P., McKenzie, D. and Singh, B. (1988) *Homeless People with Severe Mental Disorders in Inner Melbourne*. Council to Homeless Persons, Victoria.

Hirst, C. (1989) Forced exit: a profile of the young and homeless in inner urban Melbourne, Report to the Salvation Army Youth Homeless Policy Development Project.

Housing Tasmania (1988) Youth Housing Survey Report, Housing Department, February.

Howard, J. (1992) 'Taking a chance on love: risk behaviour of Sydney street youth', paper presented at the Australian Rotary Health Research Fund Fifth International Conference, Adolescent health behaviour: identifying vulnerability and resilience, Canberra, November.

Howe, B. (1985) 'Supported Accommodation Assistance Bill 1985', Hansard: House of Representatives, 27 March, 1018–22.

Human Rights and Equal Opportunity Commission (1989) *Our Homeless Children* (Burdekin Report). Australian Government Publishing Service, Canberra.

Jordan, A. (1978) *A Place of Dignity*. Australian Government Publishing Service, Canberra.

Keniston, K. and the Carnegie Council on Children (1977) *All our children: the American family under pressure*. Harcourt Brace Jovanovich, New York.

Kennedy, R. (1982) 'Charity and Ideology in Colonial Victoria', in Kennedy, R. (ed.), *Australian Welfare History: Critical Essays*. Macmillan, Melbourne.

Kilmartin, C. (1987) 'Leaving Home is Coming Later', *Family Matters*, 19 (October): 40–3.

Kozol, J. (1988) Rachel and Her Children: Homeless Families in America. Fawcett Columbine,

McDivett, I. (1986) 'Housing and Young People's Outreach: An Adjunct to Shelters', *Youth Studies*, 5 (2) (August): 36–8.

Macdonald, C. (1991) Nowhere to Go, A Review of the Housing and Support Needs of Homeless Young Pregnant Women and Young Mothers in the North East Region of Melbourne. Youth Emergency Accommodation Program, Melbourne.

Mackenzie, D. and Chamberlain, C. (1992) 'How Many Homeless Youth', *Youth Studies Australia*, 11 (summer): 14–22.

Mass, F. and Hartley, R. (1988) On the Outside: The Needs of Unsupported, Homeless Youth. Australian Institute of Family Studies, Policy Background Paper No. 7, November.

Meekosha, H. and Jakubowicz, A. (1987) 'Immigrant and Refugee Access to SAAP', in C. Chesterman (ed.), *Homes Away from Home: Research Reports*, (3) (January).

Morgan, E. and Vincent, C. (1987) 'Youth Housing Needs: Housing Questions?', *Youth Studies and Abstracts*, 6 (4): 21–3.

Morris, H. and Blaskett, B. (1992) *Learning to survive*. Brotherhood of St Laurence, Melbourne.

National Health and Medical Research Council (1991) *Health needs of homeless youth: a summary of the key issues for developing policies or providing services for young people*. Australian Government Publishing Service, Canberra.

National Housing Strategy (1991) *The Affordability of Australian Housing.* Australian Government Publishing Service, Canberra.
National Housing Strategy (1992) Housing choice: reducing the barriers, Issue Paper 6, National Housing Strategy. Australian Government Publishing Service, NSW.
National Youth Coalition for Housing (1983) General Youth Housing Policy, St Kilda, Victoria, February.
—— (1987) Singles Access to Assistance Under the 1984 CHSA.
—— (1993) NYCH Newsletter, January.
Neil, C. (1992) *Homelessness in Australia, Volume 1: An Overview.* Ministerial Advisory Committee on Homelessness and Housing, Melbourne.
Neil, C. and Fopp, R. (1992) Homelessness in Australia, Causes and Consequences, CSIRO and Victorian Ministerial Advisory Committee on Homelessness and Housing, Melbourne.
Noller, P. and Callan, V. (1991) *The adolescent in the family.* Routledge, London.
O'Connor, I. (1989) *Our Homeless Children: Their Experiences.* Report to the National Inquiry into Homeless Children by the Human Rights and Equal Opportunity Commission. Australian Government Publishing Service, Canberra.
—— (1990) 'Juvenile crime: can the Children's Court prevent further offending?' *Youth studies,* 9(3): 12–17.
O'Connor, I. and Tilbury, C. (1985) 'And the law': the legal aid needs of Australian youth', *Youth Studies Bulletin,* 4 (Nov): 17–24.
Pusey, M. (1991) *Economic Rationalism in Canberra: A Nation Building State Changes It's Mind.* Cambridge University Press, Cambridge.
Quixley, S. (1990) 'Whose Children?, Responding to Homeless Under 16 year olds. South Australian Youth Housing Network, Adelaide.
Resnick, M. (1992) The generalizability of protective and risk factors for adolescent well being. Paper presented at the Australian Rotary Health Research Fund Fifth International Conference, Adolescent health behaviour: identifying vulnerability and resilience, Canberra, November.
Robinson, C. (1992) No Visible Means of Support or . . . A Living Income, State Youth Affairs Councils and Networks, Youth Action and Policy Action, NSW.
Robson, B. (1992) Rough justice: sexual assault, homelessness and the law. NorthEast Centre Against Sexual Assault, Melbourne.
Rosenthal, D. and Moore, S. (1991) 'Adolescents and HIV AIDS: risky business', *Youth Studies,* 10 (1): 20–5.
Saunders (1990) Efficiency and Effectiveness in Social Policies: an International Perspective. Discussion Paper No. 28. Social Policy Research Centre, University of New South Wales, December.
Sheridan, G. et al. (1983) 'One Step Forward': Youth Homelessness and Emergency Accommodation. Report of the National Evaluation Committee of the Youth Services Scheme.

Bibliography 151

Sinfield, A. (1981) *What unemployment means.* Martin Robertson, Oxford.
SkillShare and Department of Employment Education and Training, (1992) Evaluation of the SkillShare Program, Some Findings, a paper presented at the SkillShare Information Days, October–December.
South Australian Youth Incomes Task Force (1988) Report (Chairperson Anna Yeatman).
Staples, P. (1992a) 'New Programs to Help Young Homeless and 'At Risk' Young People to Find Work'. Minister for Aged, Family and Health Services Media Release, PS 255/92, 27 July. Parliament House, Canberra.
—— (1992b) 'Young Homeless People to Get Help Finding Jobs'. Minister for Aged, Family and Health Services Media Release, PS 349/92, 20 October, Parliament House, Canberra.
Sullivan, L. (1992) 'AIDS update: the gap between knowledge, attitudes and behaviour', *Youth Studies,* 11 (1): 47–9.
Supported Accommodation Assistance Program (SAAP) (1990) Home for a Night. One-night Census November 1989. Commonwealth Assistance for Housing, Canberra.
—— (1991a) Home for a Night. One-night Census November 1990. Commonwealth Assistance for Housing: Canberra.
—— (1991b) Two weeks in September. Summary report on the findings of a census of SAAP funded accommodation services 17–39 September 1990. Commonwealth Assistance for Housing, Canberra.
Synott, J. (1987) Homelessness and Inadequate Housing on Thursday Island: An Ethnographic Study. Federal Department of Community Services and Health.
Tasma (Jessie Couvreur) (1890) 'Monsieur Caloche', in Spender, L. (1988) (ed.), *Her Selection.* Penguin, Melbourne.
Taylor, J. (1990) Leaving care and homelessness, Brotherhood of St Laurence, Child poverty policy review 5.
Tucker, H. (1894) *The New Arcadia.* George Robertson, London.
Tulloch, L. (1993) Enter the Gamine: out of the Gutter and on to the Catwalk. *Mode,* April–May, 18–20.
Victorian Consultative Committee on Social Development (1979) Youth Accommodation Report, 2nd edition.
Victorian Family and Children's Services Council (1991) Services for homeless young people.
Walters, S. (1982) *Homeless Youth.* Report from the Senate Standing Committee on Social Welfare. Australian Governement Publishing Service, Canberra.
White, R., (1990) *No space of their own.* Cambridge University Press, Cambridge.
White, R. Underwood, R. and Omelczuk, S. (1991) 'Victims of violence: the view from the youth services', *Australian and New Zealand Journal of Criminology,* 24 (1): 25–39.

Young, C. M. (1987) Young People Leaving Home in Australia: The Trend Towards Independence. Australian Family Formation Project, Monograph No. 9, Canberra.

Young Women's Housing Collective (1991) Do You Feel Safe Here, A Study of Young Women's Experiences in Youth Housing and Refuges, Collingwood, Melbourne.

Youth Affairs Council (1983) 'Creating Tomorrow Today', Youth Affairs Council of Australia, St Kilda, Victoria.

Youth Resource Centre (1991) AIDS: the consequences for young people, *Youth Studies*, 10 (1): 32–4.

Index

A-W = Ardoch-Windsor Secondary College

accommodation
  A-W program, 39-40, 42-3
    funding by Body Shop, 55, 69
    funding by Esprit, 40, 69
    funding by Odyssey, 40
    funding by Wesley College, 69
  crisis (refuges and shelters), 36, 37, 69, 91-3, 94, 136
  government-supported, 36-7
  inadequate support for independent, 94-5
  lack of assistance from government, 37-9
  New South Wales Youth Accommodation Association, 80
  not sole solution, 134
  number seeking (1980/81), 78
  Prahran Secondary College program, 44, 46
  private sector, 83, 84-5, 89, 95
  public housing, 84, 89, 95
  St Kilda/Prahran Student Accommodation Program, 37
  shortage, 84-5
    of medium to long term, 94
  waiting time
    in ACT, 117
    in Victoria, 36-7
  where unsupported homeless live, 1, 3, 33, 35, 36, 38, 69
  Young Homeless Allowance, 96
  see also Supported Accommodation Assistance Program (SAAP)

adolescence
  and dependence, 86
  not too late, 129, 135-8

Age article on A-W program, 60-4
ANZ Trustees support for A-W program, 40
Archdall, Vivien, 12
Ardoch Youth Foundation Inc., 10-11, 49, 51-2, 63
Ardoch-Windsor Secondary College, 12
  philosophy, 32, 63
  program, xi, 9-10, 15-31, 32-42, 60-4, 129-30, 135
    breakfast and lunch, 22, 23, 24, 29-30, 35, 51-4, 60-1, 68-9
    community support, 10-11, 35, 37, 39-40, 47-64, 69-70
    initiation, 9-10
    see also Eloise

Index

numbers in, 10, 35, 38, 62
outcomes, 19, 21, 22, 23, 24, 25-6, 27, 28-9, 30, 31, 40-2, 63, 70, 135
student stories, 1, 17-31, 33-4, 46, 61-3
Student Welfare Co-ordinator *see* Hilton, Kathy
transfer to Prahran Secondary College, 10, 41-2, 43-6
students unable to transfer, 41-2
youth worker, 38, 42-3, 44, 63, 68
see also Loughman, Mike
see also accommodation
at-risk categories, 6-7, 82, 85, 90, 138
Aborigines, 85, 90
age group/range, 89
difficulty in estimating, 82
disabled, 90
inadequate information, 15
mentally ill, 134-5
mothers, 90
non-English-speaking-background youth, 12, 90
refugees, 85
rural youth, 90
students, 10, 38, 42
Students At Risk Program (SARP), 12, 38-9, 63
wards of state, 85, 102, 115, 136
women, 6-7, 90, 107
Australian Bureau of Statistics
estimate of numbers, 81
unemployment and education, 5

Bainbridge, Trish, support for A-W program, 50-1
Bell, John, support for A-W program, 40, 47
Beth, her story, 23-4
Black, Barbara, support for A-W program, 48
Black, Leah, support for A-W program, 55

Body Shop support for A-W program, 52, 54-5, 69
Box Forest Secondary College (Glenroy) HOME program, 14-15
boys *see* men
Brotherhood of St Laurence (BSL), 12-13
Learning to Survive (Morris and Blaskett), 12-13, 109-10
support for A-W program, 35
Burdekin, Brian, 40
Burdekin Inquiry *see* Burdekin Report (1989)
Burdekin Report (1989), vi, 1-2, 4, 6-7, 9, 63, 65, 66, 67, 85, 87, 94, 103, 111-13, 125, 127
see also National Inquiry into Homeless Children
Business and Community for Young People (Esprit), 47
Byrne, John, 14

Carol, her story, 30-1
Carter, Jan, 129-44
Christine, her story, 27-9
Clare, Vaughn, support for A-W program, 11, 44, 51-2
Clayton/Huntingdale Secondary College, 12, 13
Collingwood Secondary College, 12
community
cost of homelessness, 101, 116-18
inadequate response, 1-2
involvement in programs, 11-12, 15, 39, 40, 41, 47-64, 69-70, 129, 133, 136, 140
policy options, 118-20
see also schools
Community Services Victoria, 12, 37
Conabere, Tony, support for A-W program, 11, 48-50
Corbett, Brian, 37, 39

# Index

DeCruz, Geoff, 13
deinstitutionalisation outcomes, 134-5
Dixon, Daryl, 121-8

economic benefits of support, 121-8
  increasing employability, 122
economic costs, 121-2, 127-8
  crime, 126
  employment, 123, 124-5
  income support, 123-4
  payment of benefits, 100-1, 122, 123, 125
  related to social costs, 6
  taxes lost, 122, 124
  see also social costs; unemployment
education
  and accommodation, 96-8
  AUSTUDY, 12, 97, 142
  and employment, 5, 67, 97-8, 128
  Job Replacement and Employment Program (JPET), 98
  SkillShare, 97-8
  Young Homeless Allowance, 96
  see also government; schools
Eloise, her story, 1, 10, 11, 17-19, 33-4, 52, 56, 57, 61-3, 69
employment
  and education, 5, 67, 97-8, 128
  and personal identity, 108-9
  see also unemployment
Esprit
  Business and Community for Young People, 47
  support for A-W program, 40, 47, 69
Evans, Katherine, support for A-W program, 57

family
  breakdown as cause of homelessness, vi-vii, 17-31, 34, 84, 85
  conflict as cause of homelessness, 84

  maintenance of relations with, 139
  need for support, 86, 138-9
  school as substitute, 5, 9, 58-9, 67, 71-3, 119-20, 129-30, 136-9
financial needs of students, 12-13
  see also government
Fiona, her story, 19-21
Firbank School support for A-W program, 56-7
Fopp, Rodney, 74-99

Genazzano Community support for A-W program, 50-1
General Supported Accommodation Program (GSAP), 79, 92
girls *see* women
Goodrick, Delwyn, 14
government
  AUSTUDY, 12, 110, 142
  benefits, 100-1, 122, 123, 125
  below poverty line, 108, 110
  unemployment
    low level for under-18s, 84
    withdrawal from under-16s, 84, 131, 142
  deinstitutionalisation policy, 134-5
  education, 119
  federal and state services, 2, 93
  funding, 130
    for accommodation, 36-7
    for community organisations, 92, 93
    lack, 15, 36, 37-8, 39, 58, 70, 95, 133, 134
  Homeless Students Co-ordination Project, 38
  inadequate response, 1-2, 36-8, 59, 62, 70
  Job Search Allowance (JSA), 108, 123
  Newstart, 108
  role, 70-1
  sole parent pension, 123, 125
  Students At Risk Program (SARP), 12, 38-9, 63

Index

Victorian Council of Social Service (VCOSS) review, 2
Victorian Education Department, 12
wards of state, 85, 102, 115, 136
see also economic costs; policy options; United Nations Convention on the Rights of the Child
Grace, Marty, 14
Grey, Jenny, support for A-W program, 58-9
Grundfeld, Tania, support for A-W program, 55-6

Hanover Welfare Services support for A-W program, v, 43
Harrison, Gordon, 37
Harrison, Russell, 43-5, 60, 61
Hartley, Robyn, 100-20
Hill, Margaret, 50
Hilton, Kathy, 1, 4, 11, 15, 19, 20, 22, 23, 24, 26, 32-42, 44, 46, 47, 60, 61 and *passim*
home, defined, 3-5
HOME (Holding On to My Environment) Project, 14-15
Homeless Students Co-ordination Project, 38
homelessness
 age group/range, 88-9, 104-5
 causes, vi-vii, 17-31, 34, 66, 71, 83-91, 99
  abuse and violence, vi-vii, 17-31, 66, 84, 91
  alcohol and drugs, 84
  choice, 84, 85
  exclusion from labour market, 85, 86, 89-90, 141-2, 144
  family breakdown, vi-vii, 17-31, 34, 84, 85, 86
  family conflict, 84
  institutionalisation, 84
  lack of welfare benefits, 84
  low/absent unemployment benefits, 84, 131, 142
  not choice, 66, 87-8, 111

  other, 84-5
  personal factors, 91
  poverty, 85, 86
  pregnancy, 84
  psychological, 84
  residual explanation, 6, 84, 88, 91
  solutions defined by, 95-6, 99
  school related, 84
  structural explanation, 6, 84, 85, 86, 88-91, 99
  symptoms confused with, 91
 characteristics, 2-5, 102, 103-4, 134-5
 factor in unemployment, 90, 108-9, 124-5
 in fiction, 142
 in history, 141-3
 inadequate information, 15, 70
 incidence *see* numbers
 myths *see* myths and misconceptions
 not caused by leaving home, 89
 prevention *see* prevention of homelessness
 raising awareness, 65-6, 73
 risk categories *see* at-risk categories
 stereotypes, 103, 105, 117-18
  denied, 7, 105, 108
 US experience, 71-2
 wards of state, 85, 102, 136
 younger children, 102, 105, 131, 142
 see also social costs
housing *see* accommodation
Human Rights and Equal Opportunity Commission *see* Burdekin Report (1989)

Jim, his story, 24-6
Joan, her story, 31
John, his story, 29-30

Kerrie, her story, 21-2
Kirner, Joan, 37, 62

Loughman, Mike, 15, 22, 23, 40, 42-3, 44, 45-6

Marcus, his story, 63-4
Maribyrnong Secondary College Homeless Students Project, 12, 13-14
Mary, her story, 26-7
Matt, his story, 46
men
 drug use, 114
 homelessness more visible, 6
 self-abuse, 113
 social costs of homelessness, 104, 112, 113, 114
Millar, Jen, 11
Mount Scopus Memorial College support for A-W program, 39, 48
Muller, Denis, support for A-W program, 60-4
myths and misconceptions, 35, 66-7, 84, 87-91, 96
 adolescence not too late, 129, 135-8
 bludgers, 131-2
 denial of problem, 132
 romanticism, 130-1
 welfare dependency, 133
 youth not same, 129, 130-2

National Housing Strategy data, 83
National Inquiry into Homeless Children, 1, 7, 38, 68, 81, 85, 87, 93, 125, 130, 131
 see also Burdekin Report (1989)
National Youth Coalition for Housing, 79
New South Wales Youth Accommodation Association, 80
numbers
 in A-W program, 10, 35, 38, 62
 of homeless youth, 73, 77-83
  ABS estimate, 81
  accompanying parents, 80
  difficulty in estimating, 77-8
  government estimate, 85
  increase, 126-7
  Mackenzie and Chamberlain estimate, 82, 83
  National Housing Strategy data, 83
  National Inquiry data, 81-2
  national surveys, 78-80
  National Youth Coalition for Housing data, 79
  New South Wales data, 80-1
  official estimate, 83
  state surveys, 80-1
  students, 73, 96-7
  Supported Accommodation Assistance Program (SAAP) data, 79-80, 82
  unemployed, 81
  Victoria data, 80, 82, 83
  Youth Services Scheme (YSS) data, 78
 of students in supported accommodation, 96
 trends in independent living, 87-8

Odyssey funding of student accommodation, 40

Peter, his story, 22-3
police assault/harassment, 104, 115, 118
policy options, 6, 91-6, 118-20, 127
 politics of hope, 141-4
 see also schools, advantage of school-based programs
Prahran Council, St Kilda/Prahran Student Accommodation Program, 37, 44
Prahran Secondary College
 A-W transferred to, 10, 41-2, 43-6
 characteristics, 43-4
 program, xi, 15, 44-6
  breakfast and lunch, 44-5, 60, 136
  numbers in, 10

support in school holidays, 45
young mothers, 45
student stories, 46, 63-4
students at risk, 10
Preston East Technical School, 12
prevention of homelessness, 129-30, 138-41
risk factors, 139-40
support for families, 138
see also community; schools
publications
Learning to Survive (Morris and Blaskett), 12-13, 109-10
'One Step Forward' (Sheridan), 84, 85
Our Homeless Children see Burdekin Report (1989)
reports on youth homelessness, 2, 145-52
Unemployment: The Economic and Social Costs (Dixon), 123
Victorian Council of Social Service (VCOSS), 2

Readydata support for A-W program, 51-2
Rothbart, Julie, support for A-W program, 11, 44, 52-3
Ryan, Maureen, 14

St Kilda Council, St Kilda/Prahran Student Accommodation Program, 37, 44
Salvation Army support for A-W program, 35
schools
advantage of school-based programs, 5, 9, 58-9, 67, 71-3, 119-20, 129-30, 136-9
Carnegie Foundation for the Advancement of Teaching (US) report, 71-2
characteristics of good program, 67-70, 71-3
Elizabeth re-entry program, 97
failure to assist homeless students, 2, 7-8, 34, 65, 67, 70
lack of information about programs, 15
mature-age and part-time students, 68
need for program in limited number of schools, 65
need for training, 65-6
number of students in supported accommodation, 96
percentage of homeless youth at, 73
raising awareness, 65-6
substitute for family, 5, 9, 58-9, 67, 71-3, 119-20, 129-30, 136-9
see also Ardoch-Windsor Secondary College; education; Prahran Secondary College
Shalom Unit, B'nai B'rith support for A-W program, 55
social costs, 7, 100-20, 125
abusive relationships, 104, 107, 113, 114
alcohol and drugs, 4, 104, 113-14
alienation, 116-17
anti-social behaviour, 7, 117-18
assault/harassment by police, 104, 115, 118
children of homeless, 104, 125-6
community, 101, 116-18
conflict with parents, 104
crime and violence, 4, 7, 101, 104, 113, 117-18, 126
male, 118
cumulative, 106
education, 5, 101, 109-10
health, 101, 105, 111-14, 125
HIV, 114-15, 125
STD, 104, 112
individual, 101, 105-16
instability and lack of support, 101, 102, 110
institutionalisation and imprisonment, 115
lack of love and emotional support, 4-5

Index 159

lack of opportunities/choices, 101, 110-11
lack of safe place, 111
loss of potential, 116, 117, 126
malnourishment and starvation, 4, 112
for men, 104, 112, 113, 114
personal identity, 106-8
poverty, 4, 101, 102
prostitution, 104, 114
psychological disturbance, 104, 105, 111-14
self-abuse and suicide, 104, 113, 117
related to economic costs, 6
unemployment, 101, 102, 108-9
violence and crime, 4, 7, 101, 104, 113, 117-18, 125, 126
male, 118
for women, 104, 107, 112, 113, 114, 125
younger children, 102, 105, 131
see also economic costs
South Australia Housing Trust, 95
South Australia school program, 95
South Oakleigh Secondary College Youth Housing Project, 13
numbers involved, 13
Starr, Dr Alex, support for A-W program, 59
Stevens, Sadie, 11
Streetgang, 51
Students At Risk Program (SARP), 12, 38-9, 63
students in study, 15-31
Supported Accommodation Assistance Program (SAAP), 12, 79, 92, 93-4
data, 80, 82
funding, 93-4
General Supported Accommodation Program (GSAP), 79, 92
numbers accommodated, 79
Review, 94
SAAP Mark II aims, 92-3

Women's Emergency Support Program (WESP), 79, 92
Sykes, Helen, 1-73

Tregonning, Eloise *see* Eloise
Tucker, Rev. Horace, 143

unemployment
and education, 5
and homelessness, 89-90, 91, 141-2, 144
number of homeless unemployed, 81
social cost, 101, 102, 108-9
see also economic costs; employment; social costs
United Nations Convention on the Rights of the Child, 133-4
breaches, 134
Upfield Secondary College, 12

Victoria University of Technology, 12, 14
Victorian Council of Social Service (VCOSS) review, 2

wards of state, 85, 102, 115, 136
Wearne, Peter, 37
Webster, Ruth, support for A-W program, 57-8
welfare payments *see* government
Wesley College support for A-W program, 48-50, 69
Westpac Youth Project (Footscray), 11-12
outcomes, 12
William Buckland Foundation, 14
Wise, Graeme, support for A-W program, 11, 44, 52, 54-5
women
drug use, 114
effects of sexual abuse, 113, 114
homeless, 6-7, 85
less visible than men, 6
leaving home, 87
personal identity, 107
at risk, 6-7, 90, 107
self-abuse, 113

social costs of homelessness, 104, 107, 112, 113, 114, 125
Women's Emergency Support Program (WESP), 79, 92
Wood-Bradley, Sasha, support for A-W program, 56-7

Yencken, David, 1-16, 65-73
Youth Services Scheme (YSS), 78
 evaluation, 78, 84
 intended for under-18s, 78
Youth Social Justice Strategy (YSJS)
 funding, 93